CW01558421

FRONT COVER: Alina von Keipigrafie
Model: Alina
BACK COVER: Alina von Keipigrafie
Model: Laura

 Contact:
imaginarium.magazine.13@gmail.com
Editor: Anastasia Diakidi
Editor & Designer: Anastasia Diakidi
Publisher: KDP / Self-published

Article Photos are public domain unless stated otherwise. All artists and photographers' photos used with creator's permission.

Contributors/content: Evangelia Papanikou, Marcia-Gayscone Masino, Japneet Chandoak, Helen Bakopoloulou, Yiannis Kokkinos, Jess Smith, Astil , Lynne Gallagher, Anastasia Diakidi.

CONTENTS

Imaginarium

FEATURES

ASTROLOGY

TAROT & DIVINATION

ANCIENT WISDOM

04

Dear friends of Imaginarium,

This is the first Summer Issue of Imaginarium Magazine! I hope wherever you are, you are enjoying the sunshine. I got some lovely comments from you, that you are reading the magazine in your gardens, or chilling with it and a cuppa and that made me smile. Thank you for sharing. I hope you are having a lovely time so far and I hope that your summer will be magical. So, let's welcome all those magical contributors, who are here this time.

In this issue, I welcome Alina von Keipigrafie. Thank you so much, Alina, for the interview and your beautiful photos.

I would like to also thank the Flying Dutch (Wo)Man for her amazing self-portraits (see left).

With great delight, I welcome Mary Lunnen, a brilliant coach who is helping us...blossom. Mary talks to us about her books, her life, and her coaching. Thank you so much Mary for being here and good luck with your new book!

I also welcome Jess Smith, who has written two articles for this issue. Jess is a proud mum, woman's space holder, and tarot reader from Mersea Island and she helps us set intentions with Tarot and also use Tarot in our daily spiritual practice. I hope you enjoy them both.

This time we have loads of articles about the Water. We examine the Water element, physically but also metaphysically. Its purpose in magick and divination, customs, and traditions.

Thanks once again to our regular contributor Evangelia Papanikou for her article Summer Solstice: Cursed or Blessed. I truly enjoyed that, I hope you, too.

Thanks also to Marcia Gayscone-Masino who wrote for us the article Tarot as a Healer! Extremely interesting and useful for all those who know...and don't know about tarot.

Last but not least, a special thank you to Yiannis Kokkinos for his article about the Ancient Asclepieia: Healing and Dream. I found this article very interesting and as a fellow Gemini, I enjoy Yiannis' approach and his thinking. I am sure you will like it.

If you have any feedback, please share, we appreciate it. This magazine gives voice to creative people and we'd love to hear from you. Also if you wish to submit an article or advertise your work please get in touch through the website: https://imaginariumworld.co.uk

Thank you so much for supporting the magazine because through your support as I always say we are all celebrating what makes life beautiful; art, mystery, imagination, and magic.
Thank you for everything.

Love,

Anastasia Diakidi

Photo and Model: The Flying Dutch (Wo)man

Anastasia Diakidi was born and raised in Rhodes, Greece. She studied Archaeometry and History in the Department of Mediterranean Studies at the University of the Aegean and after graduation continued her studies with Gothic Literature courses at the Phoenix Rising Academy in London, and Mysticism courses at the University of Kent. She continued with Travel Writing seminars at the University of Cambridge. Her love for astrology started at home and very early. In 2018 she started studying astrology at the "Astropaedia" in Athens and she completed her studies in 2020. She also completed her training in traditional Horary astrology with Vasilios Takos in Deborah Houlding's STA (School of Traditional Astrology). In the meantime, she attends courses, seminars and lectures by international astrologers.
She is a member of ISAR. She has been living and working in Canterbury, Kent, UK since 2012.

For astrology lessons and readings contact anastacia.d86@gmail.com or book through the website https://imaginariumworld.co.uk

BASIL OCIMUM BASILICUM

According to the legend, the Basil sprouted around the tomb of Jesus after his Resurrection, while it is said that the herb was brought to Greece by Empress Helen when she found it at Golgotha, the site of the Crucifixion.

Basil has a long tradition in every culture. There are over 60 species of basil around the world and each has a distinct smell and taste. A sacred herb in many civilizations and especially in India where it was put in royal tombs as a "passport" to the afterlife. It is believed that even common people should be buried with basil on their chests to ensure that the deceased would go to Heaven.

In India, a wreath made of basil stated that the one who wore it was a wise and holy man while they had such respect for the herb, that they swore in basil in the courts and every house in the village had its own flowerpot. In their tradition also, they used to plant basil next to the tombs of their loved ones, to call their soul to be reborn.

In ancient Egypt, women who visited the tombs to pray for the souls of the dead spread basil as a funeral offering around the sarcophagus.

To the Romans, basil was a herb of fertility and was believed to thrive only when cared for by a young unmarried girl.

The heart-shaped leaves of the herb were offered as a sign of romantic feelings in Italy. They believed that if a girl accepted a leaf of the herb from an admirer, she would fall madly in love with him; while if a man took a sprig of fresh basil from a woman, he would fall in love with her for the rest of his life.

In Italy, also, girls put a basil sprigs in their hair to declare that they were free and available, while in Romania when a boy received a basil sprig from a girl, it meant that he would be engaged.

In Tudor England, it was customary to offer basil as a sign of love while a pot of basil by the window meant that the lady of the house was expecting her lover.

In Greece, they offered a sprig of basil to the guests as a welcome or used it to create love between friends. Another Greek tradition has men putting a basil sprig in their hat on September 14th, the day of the celebration of the Holy Cross.

Basil is the birthday plant for those who have been born on the 12th July.

Basil in Herbology and folk medicine

Basil has been used since ancient times in folk medicine.
The Greeks and Romans chewed basil leaves as a sedative and used them as a decoction against digestive disorders.
It was administered both as an expectorant and as a laxative in 19th century Europe.
Basil infusion was also a common medicine against cataracts. Dried and powdered, it was ideal for irritated nasal mucosa and migraine relief.

Its therapeutic uses are numerous and among other things it helps to treat colds, migraines, bleeding, epilepsy, and scorpion bites.

The Japanese used basil decoction to treat the common cold while in India they used the same decoction for a persistent cough. Sources sometimes say that they chewed the leaves to cause salivation.

Many doctors, however, were reluctant to prescribe basil as a medicine. The famous botanist of the 17th century Nicolas Culpeper wrote that the Basil has either ardent friends or fanatical enemies.

Experienced doctors in West Africa also used it as an excellent antipyretic and the Egyptians used it along with myrrh and frankincense as a raw material in the embalming of the Pharaohs.

If you are used to drinking basil decoction you should be aware that it will cause you drowsiness. In folk medicine, it is known that goats that chew every herb never eat basil because it makes them lethargic.

Its consumption lowers blood sugar levels, harmful cholesterol, and triglycerides.
Helps with dysuria, cystitis, and urinary tract infection. Basil extract heals stomatitis and cold sores.

Basil is considered a shield of protection against madness and evil, while it was used in incense burners for exorcism and purification baths. It is no coincidence that in the Orthodox Church it is widely used in the sanctification and decoration of the Holy Table.

In aromatherapy, it is indicated for depression, stress management, nerves, insomnia, and often for lack of self-confidence, since it cleanses the head and gives clarity and strength to the spirit. It is effective in helping with stress during exams.

To be used in small quantities and to be avoided in pregnancy.

It mixes well with essential oils such as geranium, bergamot, and citrus. Its oil is effective for acne and skin problems. It is also used in allergies such as allergic rhinitis and works against intestinal pathogens and candida. It works as a natural insect repellent since its strong aroma keeps flies and mosquitoes away.

In Ayurveda it is used to increase the body's resistance to stress, to strengthen endocrine function, and is suitable for physical and mental endurance as it balances the chakras.

Photo Canva database

Basil in Witchcraft

As we have seen, the tradition of Basil extends to every culture and its uses are innumerable in both magick and traditional medicine.

Basil is a herb that loves the heat and dies in the cold of winter and that is why the witches of Greece and Anatolia took great care of it with since its flowering symbolized the flowering of their wallet.

A herb of Mars with rulership in Scorpio, it is believed that the power of the basil is doubled if it is picked on the day of the feast of St. Vasilios, hence its name (Vasilikos in Greek).

However, as Mara Meimaridis mentions in the Book of Witchcraft 1, the name of the basil comes from the myth of a Dragon with a deadly gaze, for which it was believed that the only antidote was the basil. Perhaps that is why it was inextricably linked to reptiles and was given to the rulership of Mars and Scorpio, while its use as an antidote to their bites, especially that of scorpions, was widespread. Farmers often planted basil to protect their fields as they believed that its presence and aroma repelled snakes and scorpions, a custom that probably dates back to Roman times when farmers who planted basil used to imitate the sounds of snakes so the plants will come out strong.

For witches, it is considered the king of herbs, and the presence of basil near or inside the house is believed to bring money and financial assistance. A flowerpot placed next to the door of the house has the power to invite money to cross the threshold and bring new kind-hearted friends, while at the door of a store it could attract customers and protect against theft.

Muscle Tonic

Basil leaves
Sea salt
Olive oil

Layer the ingredients in a glass container and close it airtight. After a few weeks, remove the oil and use it for tonic muscle massage.

Love Potion

In late August, fill a wide-mouthed bottle with fresh basil leaves and cover with sherry. Leave it for 10 days, drain the sherry and replace the leaves with fresh ones. Put the sherry again, leave it for another 10 days and then drain it and bottle it.

Ann Corbet, The English Wife, 1857

Blossomed Finances

Nine basil leaves in the wallet, it is believed they could call for money to make roots.

In the magical tradition, they used the oil and its powder on green candles to increase their power in financial matters. Soak basil for three days and sprinkle the water on the shop door and cash register.

Legend has it that witches used to drink half a glass of the basil juice before flying and it was also known that the juice helps with astral projection.

In the Botanical Tarot is symbolized by Two of Wands as it encourages us to recognize our true worth, to appreciate our strengths and capabilities, and to make them come true.

Cunningham in the magical encyclopaedia, says that the smell of fresh basil caused sympathy between two people and was used to calm the spirits between quarrelling lovers. It is often added to aphrodisiac mixtures and the fresh leaves, if rubbed on the skin, act as a natural erotic fragrance.

Basil is also used in love divination. It is believed that if you put two leaves of fresh basil on charcoal you will learn about the future of your relationship. If they burn quickly and stay inseparable, the relationship will be harmonious. If there are fractures the couple's life will be disrupted by quarrels while if the leaves separate with intensity and break, the relationship is not desirable.

A basil belt worn by a woman increased fertility whilst it protects a man from possible sexual problems. A potion made of basil and cardamom also ensured sexual endurance. The witches believed that a few basil leaves kept on the chest of women or placed on the pillow of dreams secured the fidelity of their partner. Alternatively, they put a powder of dried leaves on the chest. Sometimes they sprinkled the dust on their bodies while their partner slept, especially on the heart, to bless their relationship with faith.

An old recipe for labour pains said that holding a basil root in one hand along with a swallow's feather would give birth without pain.

Magick Secrets

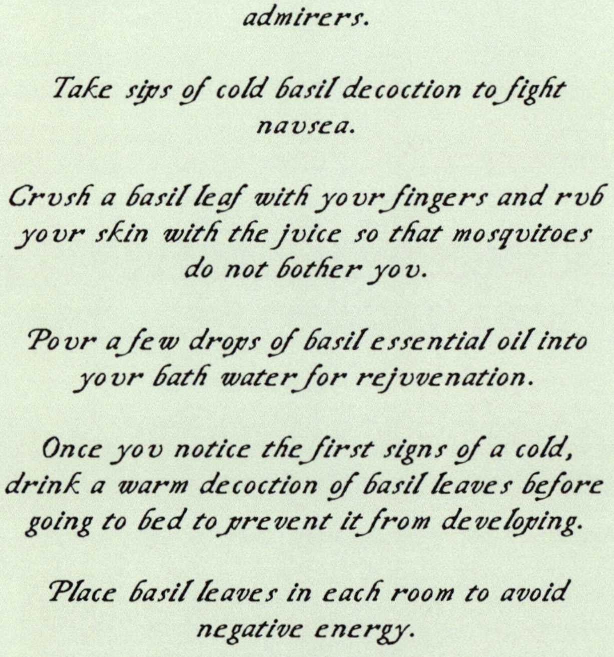

Put a pot of basil in your new home for good luck.

Grow basil in a pot to have permanent admirers.

Take sips of cold basil decoction to fight nausea.

Crush a basil leaf with your fingers and rub your skin with the juice so that mosquitoes do not bother you.

Pour a few drops of basil essential oil into your bath water for rejuvenation.

Once you notice the first signs of a cold, drink a warm decoction of basil leaves before going to bed to prevent it from developing.

Place basil leaves in each room to avoid negative energy.

If you dream that you are planting Basil, you will soon have a very important message. If you dream that you are holding basil you will have a marriage proposal and if you are newly married, you will live a happy life with your partner.
If you dream of a beautiful green fresh basil with or without its flowers, pleasant events will happen to you in the romantic field, but the withered basil means illness.

Rub a few basil leaves on the forehead when you leave the house for protection.

Basil

The strong woman is a woman who has love in her heart that could fill the hearts of those she loves and this love never ends.
The strong woman has a strong reason and honour.
The strong woman puts her words into practice because whatever she says or does, she feels it first and promises it and then acts on it.
The strong woman when she talks to you looks at you straight in the eye and her eyes reflect the truth.
The strong woman hates lying and the masks worn by two-faced people.
The strong woman is the one who seems spontaneous and expressive and so she always introduces herself to you without changing her ways.
The strong woman knows how to respect;
The strong woman is a tireless and selfless helper and can even be a shield of protection.
The strong woman doesn't try to convince anyone, she lets the obvious be known.
The strong woman achieves everything from the smallest to the greatest, but she can also do the impossible, and she wins the battles with her sword.
The strong woman walks with her head up, no matter how humiliated or belittled she feels, because her dignity and pride prevail.
The strong woman never sees others as money or as high society, but only sees them in her heart, and in the depths of her soul she respectfully embraces the values of others.
The strong woman always admires beauty and does not copy anyone because she has a strong personality and recognizes it.
The strong woman immediately recognizes her mistakes and tries to correct them with kindness and remorse.
The strong woman is recognized only by strong men and by positive people full of love and light.
the strong woman knows how to walk away with grace and kindness from the people who do not appreciate and respect her.

Woman is the symbol of strength.

The Music of the Water-King

The following story of Novgorod trader named Sadko, is a good specimen of the numerous stories of waterman and mermaids are told in Russian folklore.

One day feeling rather dreary on account of his great poverty, Sadko went down to the shore of the lake Leman and there began to play his musical instrument, the gusli. Suddenly the waters of the lake were troubled and up rose the water-King, the Tsar Morskoi, who thanked the trader for his pleasant music and promised him a reward. Sadko thereupon threw a net into the lake and drew a great treasure.

He had now become a very wealthy merchant, and one day he was sailing over the blue sea when suddenly the vessel stopped and could proceed no farther. The sailors wondered on account of whose guilt their vessel had been stopped and decided to cast lots. The lot fell on Sadko, who now confessed that he had been sailing on the sea for twelve years, but had forgotten to pay tribute to the Tzar Morskoi or Water-King. As a result, the sailors flung Sadko into the sea and their vessel could now move on. When Sadoo sank to the bottom of the sea, he found a dwelling made of wood where lay the Tsar Morskoi.

"I have been expecting thee for twelve years", said the Water King, "and am anxious to hear thee play. Begin at once."
Sadko obeyed and the Water-king was greatly pleased with the music. The Tsar Morskoi was so pleased with Sadko that as a reward he offered him the hand of any of his thirty daughters. Sadko chose the nymph Volkhof and they got married.

Angelo S. Rappoport, The sea

Dr. Edward Bach was a British Physician, who began to see disease as an end product; a final stage; a physical manifestation of unhappiness, fear, and worry. He, therefore, began to look to nature to find healing flowers. Over a period of years, Dr. Bach found 38 healing flowers and plants that with the right preparation became the 38 Bach Flower Remedies. These Remedies are enough to remove all negative emotional problems.

We will analyse the next two groups of flowers which concern the:

1. *Loneliness Issues*
2. *Hypersensitivity to Influences and Ideas*

Helen C. Bakopoulou
Bach remedies certified Therapist
email: bakoelen@gmail.com

Photo Canva database

GROUP 5

LONELINESS ISSUES

1. WATER VIOLET= Loneliness due to pride, arrogance

People who need this remedy are proud, aloof, reserved and arrogant! They wish to be left without company even when they are ill. They do not allow others to interfere in their lives, but they do not burden them with their problems either. They seldom seek advice. By receiving the remedy, they begin with humility to enjoy the company of other people. They allow themselves to be part of the social group, to make mistakes, and eventually to seek advice.

2. IMPATIENS= Impatience, haste

People are hasty and impatient; they think quickly and act on their own. They are intelligent, spontaneous, active, and productive. They are stressful and do not have enough time. They have no patience to work with others. They are quick-tempered and abrupt. By taking the remedy, people have patience, kindness, and understanding for others. They use their potential and intelligence for the benefit of all.

3. HEATHER = Self-centeredness, talkativeness, they don't like being alone

People need to constantly talk about their own issues, problems, and experiences. And they become tiresome. They seek compliments and the affection of those around them. By taking the remedy, they are helped to mature the unmet childhood needs within them for love, recognition, acceptance. When they help others, selflessly, with good intentions, the energy, attention, sympathy and love are returned to them.

GROUP 6

HYPERSENSITIVITY TO INFLUENCES AND IDEAS

1. AGRIMONY = Use a happy façade and hide true feelings from others

People hide unpleasant emotions from themselves and others by showing a fake happy carefree face. In their hearts they are afraid of getting upset when there are quarrels, fights in their environment. They are polite, pleasant, and optimistic in company. They find it difficult to express their needs or accept gifts or help. They try to appear strong and successful. They often resort to alcohol, cigarettes, overwork, drugs, medication. By taking the remedy, their inner tension is softened, their inner torment is relieved, they feel freer to be themselves.

2. CENTAURY= weakness of will, cannot say no

People have a weak will and cannot say no to whatever is asked of them. They allow themselves to be exploited without protest. They are afraid to raise their voice, to argue, to resist. They are quick to compromise. They work too hard because they desire recognition and value. They are easily influenced by others. By taking the remedy, they are helped to strengthen their will, to discern when to say no and when to say yes; to maintain their own identity and not to be servile and enslaved by others.

3. WALLNUT= For transitions and major changes in life

People find it difficult to adapt to changes. Whether it's a job, a new environment, a new home, a new country, a divorce, or quitting smoking. This remedy helps people to take the next step towards the big decision in their lives and not to be attached to their present situations.

4. HOLLY= Hatred, envy, jealousy, suspicion, cruelty

People feel jealousy, hatred, envy, and revenge. They suffer a lot within themselves for their misery. They often feel hurt and wronged. They suspect that they have been cheated. They are not aware of how to love themselves because they have turned away love and at the same time they feel the danger of losing it. By taking the remedy, they open their heart and drive away fear. They realize that we are all children of universal Love. The heart opens and sees others as brothers and sisters and they become able to feel happy for the successes of others even when they have problems.

Summer

By Japneet Chandoak

The clouds are shifting, it's starting to rain,
Never have I ever outstretched my hand, to let it fall over me,
This feeling of water is strange, I've always shed my own when it rained,
For the first time, it rains with love, not melancholy.
Never had you ever taken the leap, grabbed my hand and danced with me.
Slipping on the wet ground, but yet not quite falling,
Your arms around me, forever cautious, oh, to love and to be loved.
So used to drowning, the possibility of swimming never crossed my mind,
Now we're throwing pool parties, this lavender haze is divine.
Even when the clouds are grey, the darkness so heavy it engulfs me whole,
You've made me your sun, your everlasting glory,
Different from the star I'd always been, trapped in the love affair of the moon,
The one they'd die for, but still always the other women in my own tale,
I've always failed, failed to be whole,
But with a piece of you, covering my scars, a human bandage,
I don't bleed anymore, the ache feels old,
Flowers bloom in all your directions, how does it feel to walk the earth,
Barefoot, floating, with no gravity to support you.
How does it feel to bring me this gold rush, every time I look at you?
Because it never rusts, it never ages, it stays the same,
A glimpse of you is an eternity of dancing in the rain.

Photo Canva database

So scarlet it was, maroon

Leave handprints all across you,
My fingers scarlet with your love,
Drop by drop I fall,
But I'm just a ripple in your ocean,
The waves so strong, you became a tsunami,
But I was never even a storm,
It's all quiet now, but I have much to say,
I write all my curses down using the same paper I wrote you my love,
But I throw it all out, burn the paper, burn it all,
How do you burn memories away?
Get the pictures, get the poems, erase all trace.
What do I do with your ashes?
They're sitting in the urn, lying on my coffee table,
Its leg's still taped from the night you pushed me and I fell,
I'm just clumsy, I never learnt how to walk the right way.
Remember the night I held you while your tears escaped?
I'm sitting in the same spot, the floor's a little cold but I tore my blanket to shreds,
Search for firewood, burn it all, but I see us dancing in the flames,
Try to reach out and grab us, but there's just blinding hot pain,
I know this agony, we call it love.
Red-rimmed roses, the same shade as the knife in my skin,
Carve me away to your liking, I see no scars, just love marks,
Marked me for eternity, I can no longer recognise myself,
The mirror whispers of a version I've always dreamt of, the blood moon right overhead,
Walk by our pictures in frames and into the night,
In one of them, we looked so happy and you held me so tight,
Raking your nails all over my frame, drawing out your love from my veins,
So scarlet it was, maroon.

I want to know how it feels to be water.

by Lynne Gallagher

I want to know how it feels to be water. Know how it feels when molecules rearrange, miraculously contorting into myriad forms. Imagine the freedom of fluid transformation, being able to know every part of the land, seas, and atmosphere. A living being with memory, existing everywhere all at once.

So often we forget, perhaps never consider, the ways that water exists. Part of every being, essential to form and survival, living in the atmosphere, major element of the human body, covering the planet with a blue mantle that marks us out in the universe as a place of life. Our experience of her mundane, used to the steady flow from the tap, seeing her as ordinary, nothing more than a way to satiate our thirst. Water is so much more. Imagine for a moment being her. Imagine the journeys she has taken to end in your glass.

Begin at the top of the world. The great Himalayas, source of the major rivers on the planet. Imagine the cold air, water vapour cooled until it forms clouds, vast and heavy as more vapour solidifies into that misty state prior to becoming a fully fledged droplet. Being buffeted by billions of others all vibrating, awaiting that moment of change. Finding a form that hurls itself gleefully towards the earth. And they must be gleeful, don't raindrops dance? Feeling the freedom of release cavorting and plummeting headlong to the ground below, hitting mountains, running down rocks, racing through deep crevices formed by those gone before. Announcing their presence as they reverberate from the surfaces of all they touch. Shouting so loudly they alert the sun who peeks through the dwindling clouds illuminating them into a show of brilliance. Each drop a prism reflecting colour, and just at the right moment joining together, becoming rainbow. A demonstration of their versatility, bringing joy to the grey sky. No wonder they dance.

Onward they go, down to the surface. Some sucked gratefully into the earth to feed the beings deep within, others run in tiny torrents from leaves into the swirling waters of rivers. Reuniting with others they knew before, becoming part of the wild current that dashes against rocks carving its path, making its mark for others to follow, molecules on the wildest ride any theme park could imagine. Onward, rushing over boulders brought along for the ride by ancestors as the glaciers melted, the slow moving solidity creeping silently ever onward until it performs its exquisite swan dive into the waiting waters. Each molecule free at last after thousands of years static in ice form, crashing and roaring in ecstatic dance as humongous communities free fall into the expectant sea. Rapturously applauded by their waiting fans who hurl themselves into the air as mighty explosions of spray exhilarated by the spectacle. Oh, how wonderful it must feel to find warmth, to be freed from captivity and allowed to mingle with family long since forgotten. Freed from the role of spectator, allowed to once more

Each drop a prism reflecting colour, and just at the right moment joining together, becoming rainbow. A demonstration of their versatility, bringing joy to the grey sky. No wonder they dance.

transform into something new.

Imagine the joy as the newly transformed join the tract of fresh water buoyed by their salty brethren, travelling towards new adventures, new possibilities. Bathing in the warmth of the sun as it heats the whole, some choosing to transform back to vapour and repeat the ride. Adrenaline junkies cyclically experiencing the rush. Others decide on joining the salty waters, experiencing the vibrations of waves, discovering all manner of creatures dwelling within the safety and security of their conglomeration. Those who remain buoyed upon the backs of their salty form journey onwards towards estuaries where they merge with others of their kind. Flowing with the life blood that sustains those living on the surface. Free of the influence of mother moon they find space to just be. Becalmed in lakes and ponds, gently moving rivers and canals, dwelling in peace. Experiencing the presence of fish and mammals, birds and man. Man, who constructs systems to move the waters from nature to artificial reservoirs and pipes, convenient for his needs. Water trapped in the darkness, unable to transform, unable to own her identity. Forced by pressure to rush headlong into pipes and tanks where she waits to be released, imprisoned. Cruelly heated but not enough to evaporate and escape, funnelled through taps, chemicals added, her form corrupted. Made heavy as she shoulders the waste and is sent onward through sewers and pipes. Others brought to a different fate run into cups they begin the journey through human bodies.

How does it feel to be swallowed? Sent into an alien world that reduces you to atoms, destroys everything you are. Mingling with acids becoming part of a filthy soup of excretions. Your substance needed to fill the spaces in cells, to transport the waste gases as you exchange your oxygen, retaining just enough to carry the things that need to be removed out into the world. No longer bright rainbows just thick, pungent yellow poison. Ejected outwards, feeling the rush of air as you emerge, oxygen rushing into you ousting the carbon dioxide and others who hijacked your purity. Finding yourself back in the waiting arms of others of your kind, who hold you and take away the concentrated toxins dispersing them, knowing how it feels to be corrupted. Onward you travel back through pipes and filters, the toxins removed by bacteria who gratefully accept. Returning to the quiet waters resting from the shared ordeal.

Unperturbed, water craves the rush of transformation, excitedly returning to thrill seeking she waits to leap forth into the air as rain brings those she knew before, welcoming them with a ballet of joy stretching outwards wherever drops land. Beautiful ripples buoyed by the ones drawn to see the show. Ecstasy. The surface illuminated with tiny jewelled fractals of colour, remnants of light caught within the bodies of the dancers as they dove headlong to the earth. Vibrations setting currents in motion in the hidden depths. Sharing the excitement with those too far down to see it live. Alerting fish to the influx of oxygen, that invigorates the whole with new energy and brings her roaring to life.

Cycles repeating all over the planet, waters moving constantly. Transforming, never still for long, even the stillest ponds a hive of activity on a summers day as those basking on the surface wait until optimum heat is achieved and they rise into the sky, unseen, voyaging

Looking at my glass I see wonders, this once ran through the foothills of Nepal, crashed into the sea in the Arctic. Danced on the surface of the Amazon, tickling the faces of jaguars as they drank their fill. Whales have hunted and migrated thousands of miles in the very liquid that now is contained in this vessel.

high into the atmosphere. Freed from all constraints they float thousands of feet up, drawn to the warmth of the sun. A bit like Icarus, flying too close they meet with clouds, whose coolness settles their wanderlust and keeps them safe within the misty form. Unable to soar they settle into the vibrations of the whole, awaiting the moment when they become so intense they are sent as rain to cool the hot earth in new locations decided by the winds.

Such constant activity, never still, metamorphosing, remaking. How can she sustain such ruthless change? From solid to gas, extremes yet one. It fatigues my brain to even try to comprehend how she maintains such relentless transformation. Would my body survive such extremes? I seriously doubt it could. The notion of entering another being to be used as waste disposal repulses me, knowingly being the transport for poisons terrifies me. But this is her job, done without complaint, for every creature, bird, plant, fish and mammal. Every molecule travelling through each being at some point in time.

Looking at my glass I see wonders, this once ran through the foothills of Nepal, crashed into the sea in the Arctic. Danced on the surface of the Amazon, tickling the faces of jaguars as they drank their fill. Whales have hunted and migrated thousands of miles in the very liquid that now is contained in this vessel. Rainbows live in its inconspicuous clarity, ones I saw as a child? Perhaps. I am in awe of this ordinary element, that weaves her magic quietly, watching with joy as her children dance in celebration of the true wonders she performs. This one small glass holding all that is, has been and will be. The world in my hands. A mind blowing thought that this water I drink now will flow through me and in time through my descendants, as it did from my ancestors to me. The magnitude of this realisation far more than I expected, perhaps fuelled by the wisdom contained in the molecules carried from wise ones who understood more clearly than I. I wanted to know how it feels to be water, to understand her more deeply. I am transformed by the realisations I found. Captivated by her and deeply in debt for all she is. Grateful for each drop that passes through me on its journey of joy.

Lynne is a Shaman and Meditation teacher based in Birr, Co.Offaly, Ireland.

She has been practicing and teaching for over 20 years. She began her training as a shaman in 2002 under the tutelage of indigenous Peruvian shamans, adding Reiki and meditation coaching to compliment her shamanic healing techniques.

She runs meditation classes, and workshops, and holds Shamanic healing consultations, training courses and one to one sessions, in person and online.

Shamanism is her passion, she feels truly blessed to witness the transformation of her clients as she gently guides them through their healing journey. This is her lifelong learning path, to which she is constantly adding new skills to enhance the healing experience.

Complimenting her Shamanic work, Meditation coaching and teaching brings balance and harmony, giving clients the techniques they can use to combat stress and anxiety, and learn to rebalance their bodies.

Mary Lunnen Dares to Blossom

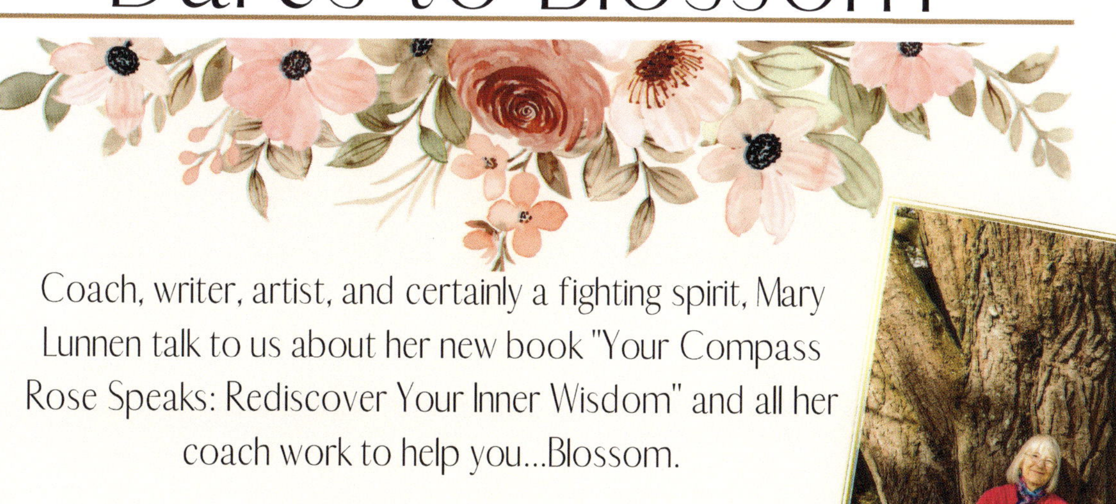

Coach, writer, artist, and certainly a fighting spirit, Mary Lunnen talk to us about her new book "Your Compass Rose Speaks: Rediscover Your Inner Wisdom" and all her coach work to help you...Blossom.

Interview to Anastasia Diakidi

A.D. Hello Mary, welcome to Imaginarium! It is wonderful to have you here sharing space with us. I would like you to tell us a few words about you and your story.

M.L Thank you, Anastasia, it is wonderful to be here. Where shall I begin? 'A few words' is a challenge. I have always loved colour and words. My mother was a creative person and encouraged me to explore making too.

I live just inland from the coast of north Cornwall, in the far southwest of the UK. My husband and I recently celebrated our 46th wedding anniversary, and in 2022 I was seventy. Neither of those things seem possible - we both imagine we are the young people who met and fell in love all those years ago.

We have no children but have always shared our home with at least one cat, currently two sisters called Evie and Edie. My husband grows a lot of our own vegetables, and we have hens who keep us supplied with fresh eggs.

A.D. How lovely, Mary. Congratulations for your anniversary, too! So, you recently published your sixth book, *Your Compass Rose Speaks: Rediscover Your Inner Wisdom*, what is the book about and what inner purpose has it come to serve? I strongly believe that every book satisfies something within us, before our wish to share something with the world. What do you think?

M.L. Thank you. Well, this book is a distillation of all my work helping people dare to blossom and rediscover their inner wisdom over the last twenty years since I set up my coaching practice, Dare to Blossom Life Coaching.

The book takes the reader on what the people I connect with often call 'a turn around the Compass Rose', beginning in the centre point, in Peace, visiting each direction, and then returning to where we began. I truly believe that this has helped me remain grounded and balanced in myself and then to step out into the world without feeling buffeted by outside forces.

Yes, I agree that 'every book satisfies something within us, before our wish to share something with the world' – writing this book (which took a number of years) has helped me see and celebrate what has emerged for me over this time, and how I have grown into and recognised my own wisdom.

A.D. Thank you for sharing all this. How interesting. Given the opportunity, you also have five more books published, would you like to tell us more about those?

M.L. It has been quite a journey, and one that looking back, I could summarise as a desire to connect with others. My first book, 'Flying in the Face of Fear: Surviving Cervical Cancer' – grew from my experience of that disease, and my own need to speak to other women who had been through it too.

There seemed to be nothing available when I was diagnosed in 1994, so after a while I compiled a book of the stories submitted by other women who wanted to share to help others. Each of us has a unique experience, and yet we all have something in common.

After that I was commissioned in 2010 (with a second edition in 2018) to write a book for a series of 'Need2Know Books' on Cervical Cancer.

And I also self-published three others: 'Dare to Blossom: Coaching and Creativity' in 2008, which takes the reader through some simple life-coaching exercises. Next was a Companion Guide to the Dare to Blossom Rediscovery Cards, that I will speak more about in a moment, and then my memoir: 'The Powerful Voice of the Quiet Ones: Reflections on an Introvert's Life'.

Originally, I thought the memoir writing would be part of 'Your Compass Rose Speaks', but – as I find books often do – that work had a mind of its own and wanted to be a standalone book. So, I self-published it in January 2020.

This latest book, 'Your Compass Rose Speaks' took a very long time to come about, with several stops and starts. I had two breakthrough moments: one when Nick Williams (author of 'The Work You Were Born to Do', and many other books), offered me a coaching session – during which the structure of the book and the chapter titles began to emerge. I am very grateful to Nick, and honoured that he agreed to write the Foreword for the book.

The second breakthrough was when I was introduced to a small publisher, Alice Maldonado Gallardo, of the Golden Dragonfly Press based in Amherst, Massachusetts, USA. Alice offered me a publishing contract and it was wonderful to have the benefit of her expertise and graphic design skills to produce the beautiful book that was published on 28th February 2023.

Signed copies are available direct from me, or of course people can order from any bookseller. There will also be a Kindle version available soon, and I am gradually recording the full text for an Audible book as well.

A.D. And you have the Dare to Blossom Rediscovery Cards. What are they? How do they work?

M.L. Yes, the first deck of cards came to me as an idea in 2011, and at first I thought 'Who am I to produce yet another set of cards?' I have a big collection, ranging from the original Angel Cards, to all sorts of oracle decks with beautiful art work. However, I know that when an idea appears, it is my responsibility to do something with it, to bring it into the world. At first, I used them in my workshops, then people asked to buy their own sets and they became available in 2012.

Each card is simply a word, on a coloured background. The principle is that through using them you will rediscover your inner wisdom – which I believe is always there but sometimes drowned out by the noise and busyness of everyday life. They work by encouraging people to notice their first response. Often, because they are so simple, so direct, that response is first felt in the body rather than the mind, and that has a powerful message. And that response will be different the next time you see that same card.

For a long time, I resisted writing the Companion Guide because I didn't feel it was for me to 'tell' anyone how to interpret the cards. Eventually I was persuaded that it would be helpful for people to have a structure, some prompts to follow. By then I had been running the 'Dare to Blossom into Joy' Facebook group for some time and people there kindly allowed me to share some of their responses to each word – to demonstrate that there is no right or wrong answer, simply today's response.

Then, in 2022, people began asking if I would produce a second deck of 50 cards (I now call these the No. 2 Deck, to distinguish them from the Original Deck) – I realised afterwards that it was exactly ten years between them. It is interesting how the two

Green Sprite by Mary Lunnen

decks have a different energy to them, even though I use mine (for myself and in groups) all mixed together in a big dish.

A.D. Dare to Blossom is your life coach name, I would like to know more about your coaching and this beautiful name you chose for your services.

M.L. Thank you – I love the name too, it is both an inspiration, and a challenge! The words Dare to Blossom emerged over time as I was completing my life coaching training. It was prompted by a card that is still on my cork board beside my desk, with that well-known quote: "...and then the day came when the risk to remain tight in a bud was more painful than the risk it took to blossom." (usually attributed to Anais Nin, although I recently read that it could be by Elizabeth Appel.)

My coaching services are all on Zoom, I was already familiar with working this way before the pandemic. I offer one to one and group programmes. My coaching training was very practical, helping people identify their goals and create an action plan to achieve their aims. Those techniques are often part of what I offer now – and I feel I have over the years developed a big 'tool box' of different things I can offer people, finding the ones that work best for them.

From 2003 to 2015 I was also employed as a business coach and trainer working with people who were starting their own businesses or becoming self-employed. This was wonderful experience and brought me in contact with a big range of different people who may not have come for private coaching. When the second of those projects came to an end I chose to focus on my own business – and that has enabled me to develop my skills more broadly and deeply, with a strong spiritual element.

A.D. You are also an artist! Multi-talented and creative! Would you like to tell us more about your artwork and where could we find it?

M.L. My parents were multi-talented and creative too and I grew up loving colour and making things. In fact, my first business that I ran, from the late 1970s to the 1990s, was making craft products such as copper enamel jewellery, silk scarves, and encaustic art. I developed arthritis in my hands which made crafts more difficult (and life moved on, as it does) – but I kept the encaustic art kit. So, when I had more time, after 2015, I was able to return to this. It is a way of 'painting' with molten wax, which creates abstracts in glowing colours. They can be like seeing pictures in a fire – the images change each time you look, and each person sees something different. You can view paintings for sale on the Dare to Blossom website here:

https://www.daretoblossom.co.uk/about/artwork

I am also an amateur photographer, and love sharing photos of my walks on the stunning cliffs and beautiful beaches near my home in north Cornwall, in the far southwest of the UK.

Mary Lunnen by Debbie Murt

A.D. I would like to ask about the workshops and events you organise. What is coming up this season?

M.L. Thank you for asking, all my events and programmes are online at the moment. This works beautifully and means that people can join from wherever they are in the world. In a recent circle on Zoom there were people from Australia and the USA as well as all over the UK.

I run several six week programmes each year, all with the underlying theme of the Compass Rose: we begin in Week 1 in Peace, then visit each direction, and come back to Return to Peace in Week 6. There is often another theme too (such as 'Weaving Shadow and Light' or 'The Key to Your Inner Wisdom', or 'Be Powerfully Yourself'. Then I offer weekly and daily prompts in a private Facebook group, and we meet each week in a Zoom Circle.

There are also occasional shorter, four-week, programmes in between these. The next is starting in the week beginning 19th June, with two taster circles, on Wednesdays 7th and 14th June. The theme is "Space to Be: Space to Breathe."

In the live gatherings on Zoom I open and close with the short meditation poem 'Your Compass Rose Speaks', then draw Dare to Blossom Rediscover Cards for each of us and take us on a Magic Carpet Ride guided visualisation. I create a quiet, safe, sacred space where people know they can share as much or as little as feels right for them at that time.

I have described the components – and, I often say that the true magic happens in the gaps. In the cards drawn for someone else that bring a message for you; in the words someone uses to describe their magic carpet ride that illuminate something in your life; and in the connections and friendships that develop over time. In fact, I also host a monthly Zoom circle for anyone who has ever joined one of the paid programmes, called 'Stay Connected' – where we do just that, and catch up as well as meeting new people.

For anyone who would like to dip a toe in to experience how this might all work, I also offer two monthly Dare to Blossom Circles, one near the beginning of the month on a Saturday at 11.00 am, and one near the end, on a Monday evening at 7.30 pm (UK times). There is no set fee, simply an invitation to offer a donation if your circumstances allow, and a warm welcome in any case.

Whenever I am inviting people to enrol in a paid programme, I offer a one or two Taster Circles, where people can ask any questions as well as experiencing the magic of a live gathering. And, if people would prefer to chat one to one, I am happy to arrange a Zoom call at a time to suit us both.

A.D. I will close with my favourite question, Mary, as I believe with this question you get something very unique from each person. So, where is magic in your life?

M.L. I am smiling Anastasia, I have used that word, magic, numerous times in this interview already. And, this is an excellent question, where is the magic in my life?

My immediate response is - in nature. Whether out on the cliffs and beaches a short drive from my home here in Cornwall, in the woods and hidden valleys inland, visiting the grand gardens around our county, or simply in my own garden – my connection with the natural world around me is what keeps me grounded and balanced, brings me joy, and peace, and always a sense of awe and wonder.

One especially powerful example is watching the fulmars swooping in the air currents on the cliffs,

I often say that the true magic happens in the gaps. In the cards drawn for someone else that bring a message for you; in the words someone uses to describe their magic carpet ride that illuminate something in your life; and in the connections and friendships that develop over time.

sometimes flying close at eye level and seeming to look straight at me with curiosity.

A.D. I wish you all the best with your new book and all your future endeavours. Thank you so much for being here with us.

M.L. Thank you. And remember step into the magic and dare to blossom, if not now, then when?

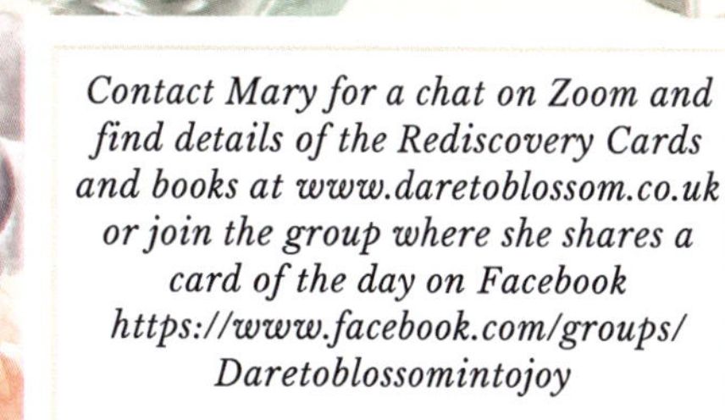

Contact Mary for a chat on Zoom and find details of the Rediscovery Cards and books at www.daretoblossom.co.uk or join the group where she shares a card of the day on Facebook https://www.facebook.com/groups/Daretoblossomintojoy

Website
www.daretoblossom.co.uk
Direct links: Signed copies of my books https://daretoblossom.co.uk/about/books

You can view paintings for sale on the Dare to Blossom website here www.daretoblossom.co.uk/about/artwork

Facebook
Mary Lunnen
& Daretoblossomart

RECIPES FROM LITERATURE

How was Aunt Isabelle making the Tipsy Cake? What's the magical recipe of Courage Tea by Maria Owens? How was Vianne making the amazing mocha in the book Chocolat? Let's organise an afternoon tea with literary recipes!

Tipsy Cake

By Aunt Isabelle from the Book The Rules of Magic

" "It's the most chocolaty chocolate you'll ever taste,""

Early alcohol-infused cakes in the U.S. were often rum cakes. Pirates sustained themselves with rum cakes on Caribbean voyages, and rum later became popular as a replacement for vanilla extract in the South. The alcohol is behind the tipsy cake's name.

1 cup unsweetened cocoa powder, plus more for dusting the pan (see note)
1 cup freshly brewed coffee
cup dark rum
1 cup unsalted butter, cut into small pieces
2 cups sugar
2 cups all-purpose flour
1¼ teaspoons baking soda
teaspoon salt
2 large eggs
cup buttermilk
1 teaspoon vanilla extract Confectioners' sugar, for dusting (optional)

CHOCOLATE RUM ICING
cup semisweet chocolate morsels
2 tablespoons butter
2 tablespoons milk or half-and-half, plus more as needed
2 tablespoons dark rum

Prepare the cake: Preheat oven to 325 F. Grease a large Bundt pan, and dust with flour or cocoa powder. Place coffee, dark rum, butter and cocoa powder in a saucepan over medium heat, and whisk gently until the butter is melted. Remove from the heat and add the sugar, stirring until dissolved. Set aside to cool.

Place the flour, baking soda and salt in a large bowl.
In a medium bowl, mix together the eggs, buttermilk and vanilla. When the chocolate mixture has cooled, stir it into the egg mixture. Add the flour mixture and whisk until well combined.
Pour the batter into the prepared pan and bake for 40 to 50 minutes, or until a toothpick inserted in the centre of the cake comes out clean. Place on wire rack to cool.
Prepare the chocolate rum icing: Melt the chocolate morsels in the top of a double boiler. Add butter, milk and rum, and simmer for 5 minutes, stirring constantly. Add more milk to thin the sauce, if necessary. Remove the sauce from the heat and allow to cool slightly.
When the cake has cooled, invert it onto a wire rack placed over parchment or wax paper. Dust with confectioner's sugar, if desired. Drizzle with chocolate rum icing. Makes 12 to 14 servings.

Recipe from Judy Gelman.

Courage Tea

Book The Rules of Magic, by Alice Hoffman

"They mixed henna with limes, roses,tea, and eucalyptus and let it simmer overnight, for henna's hue reflects the strength of love of a woman for a man, the thicker and deeper the colour, the more genuine the love. Amulets that carried apple seeds were made in the evenings as they sat out in the yard, meant to bring the wearer love, for apples signify the heart. For those who wished to gain willpower, and say no to a lover who would bring only heartbreak, there was a cure of rosemary and lavender oil. Bathe in it, and when you next saw the one you had once cherished, you would send him packing. They now had the recipe for fever tea, composed of cinnamon, bayberry, ginger, thyme, and marjoram, and for frustration tea, a combination of chamomile, hyssop, raspberry leaf and rosemary, which Jet brewed for her sister in the mornings so that the day will go smoothly. Aunt Isabel refused to hand over the formula for courage tea. That she said, was one recipe you had to discover for yourself".

Apple Turnovers

Book Little Women, by Louisa May Alcott

"There was a momentary lull, broken by Hannah, who stalked in, laid two hot turnovers on the table, and stalked out again. These turnovers were an institution, and the girls called them 'muffs', for they had no others and found the hot pies very comforting to their hands on cold mornings".

Makes approx. 8
Ingredients
6 granny smith apples, cored and peeled
3 tbsp raw caster sugar
2 sheets puff pastry
1 1/2 tsp ground cinnamon
1/2 tsp ground nutmeg
1/2 tsp sea salt1 tbsp butter, melted
2 tbsp water

Preheat the oven to 180C and prepare 2 baking trays with baking paper or by greasing them well. Dice the apples very finely, they shouldn't be more than a cm large. Place them into a medium sized saucepan along with 2 tbsp water, 1 tbsp raw caster sugar, 1 tsp cinnamon, 1/4 tsp sea salt, and 1/4 tsp of nutmeg. Cook on medium until apples have softened and the water have caramelised a little. Remove from the heat before the apples become too squishy. Combine the remaining sugar, spices and salt together and mix well. Put to the side till later. Lay the two sheets of puffy pastry out, slice each down the middle diagonally, and then again in each corner. In the end you should have 8 triangles of pastry. Spoon the apple mix onto one side of the triangle, folding the other edge over and pressing the edges closed with the prongs of a fork. Repeat with all triangles of pastry and transfer to the baking tray. Using a fork poke a few holes in the top of each, and brush well with the melted butter. Sprinkle the sugar and cinnamon mix on top before baking for around 15 minutes or until the top of the pastry is golden and brown. Enjoy!

Mocha

Book Chocolat by Joan Harris

"Armande plumped into the chair and took her glass in both hands. She looked eager as a child, her eyes shining, her expression rapt. "Mmmm." It was more than appreciation. It was almost reverence. "Mmmmmm." She had closed her eyes as she tasted the drink. Her pleasure was almost frightening.

"This is the real thing, isn't it?" She paused for a moment, bright eyes speculatively half-closed. "There's cream, and - cinnamon, I think - and what else? Tia Maria?" "Close enough," I said. "What's forbidden always tastes better anyway."

Serves 1

Ingredients

1tbsp ground coffee
1/4tsp ground cinnamon
75g good quality chocolate
50mL whipping cream
Pinch of sweet paprika
Dash of Kahlua
Chocolate shavings and a pinch of cinnamon (to decorate)

1. Make a shot of espresso, as strong as you can. Add the cinnamon into the ground coffee before you put it into whatever machine you use to make a brew.
2. Break your chocolate into pieces and place into the jug. Pour the hot coffee over the chocolate and allow it to melt. Don't stir until most of the chocolate has been incorporated into the coffee. Once it has come together, stir quickly until you're sure that all the chocolate has melted.
3. Whisk the cream by hand in a bowl until soft peaks form. Set aside until you're ready to serve the mocha.
4. Add the Kahlua and paprika to the mocha and stir. Warm the mixture over a saucepan of simmering water, or a direct flame if your jug can stand it. Once hot, pour into a glass or mug, and top with a large spoonful of the cream, the chocolate shavings and a sprinkle of cinnamon. Serve immediately.

WATER

The Element of Love

The four elements of fire, earth, air, and water are present all around us. The ancient Greeks believed that every living organism is made of a combination of these elements. It is no coincidence that the four elements have a place not only in the physical world but also in many religious concepts as well as in the metaphysical world. In this issue, we will explore the element of water.

Water is a natural element and its presence on earth allows manhood to survive and thrive. The element of Water has been linked in the physical and metaphysical world with Life itself. Because of this connection to Life, Water has been a profound symbol of motherhood and emotion.

As an element in metaphysics, it is considered passive as water symbolizes feminine qualities. In astrology, water is associated with the planets that have a moist nature, such as the Moon, while the signs that correspond to it are Cancer, Scorpio, and Pisces.

In Cancer, we see the womb, this safe moist environment where our life begins and it allows us to grow and thrive. In Scorpio, the Water has become the element that allows us to thrive and transform ourselves by facing our fears and our need for security. While, in Pisces, the Water is now a connection to the Great Mind, the great source that keeps the whole humanity connected, as children born from one some womb.

In astrology also the element of water is associated with characteristics such as sensitivity, nurturing, intuition, protectiveness, artistic tendencies, psychic sensitivity, privacy, compassionate service, and empathy. The negative characteristics of water include cowardice, over-protection, fear, escapism, secrecy, delusions, and indecisive behaviour.

As with any element, balance is everything. Water is a powerful element that allows everything to live and grow but it can be destructive and too hard to control. The same is true in human temperaments, where the element of water also needs balance, or else the negative characteristics of the element could damage the personality and those around us, especially due to excessive passivity and dependence on others.

In traditional astrology, the Water has three rulers: the Moon, Mars and Jupiter. The triplicity of Water according to Dorotheus is ruled by Mars during the Night (both Day and Night by Ptolemy and William Lily while for Dorotheus Venus is Day ruler of the Water Triplicity) and the Moon. It is interesting to examine why the ancient astrologers placed Mars as a Water triplicity ruler but this is not relevant to the present article.

In modern astrology, we do not use the triplicity rulers anymore and generally we, nowadays, connect the qualities of the water to the Moon, Venus and Neptune. The modern ruler of Scorpio is Pluto (instead of Mars) and the modern ruler of Pisces is Neptune (instead of Jupiter).

In tarot, the element of water is associated with the Cups of the Minor Arcana. As in astrology, the Cups are associated with emotions, the subconscious, compassion, and energy of the Yin. We see the power of love, protection and pleasure as well as happiness in this suit. In Major Arcana, the element of Water can be connected to the cards of the Moon, the High Priestess, the Chariot and the Hanged man.

The herbs associated with the water element have usually moisture nature such as Aloe Vera. Other herbs and flowers related to the water element are: milk thistle, water lily, verbena, echinacea, mugwort, horseradish, peppermint and spearmint etc.

In crystal healing, water-related crystals could be white in colour such as, for example, moonstone; or blue such as blue aragonite or aquamarine; or green and purple, such as amazonite and amethyst respectively. Water element crystals are known for their ability to strengthen our intuition, connect us with our psyche and balance the bodily fluids. They are often important helpers in mental health issues and in strengthening our emotional plane.

The water element corresponds to the sacral chakra. The Svadhisthana chakra relates to the water element, and like water, the sacral energy

controls fluidity, versatility, and freedom, whether sexual, emotional, or creative. When in balance, someone feels an abundance of creativity and pleasure. When out of balance, a person feels emotionally unstable, sexual dysfunction, and a lack of creative energy.

The water element in witchcraft is the use of water for magickal purposes. This includes scrying, mirror magic and relationship magic. As tools are used the cauldron, the cup or chalice, and the mirror.

Spells and rituals associated with water have to do with enhancing psychic powers, bring love to someone's life or boost fertility. Rituals involving water, such as ritual baths or anointing with tears, are also related to the element. Witches use water to cleanse and purify their energies and to connect with the element's loving and nurturing aspects. Water also plays a role in creating potions and magical teas, emphasizing its transformative and life-enhancing attributes.

Wiccans use the elements to symbolize the four directions. The four directions correspond to the four classical elements. Water is represented by lakes, streams, rivers, oceans, and rain, and is beneficial due to its cleansing, purifying, healing and nourishing qualities.

Water is the element of the west. This element is most powerful at dusk. A powerful junction point between solar and lunar energies, dusk is the time when the portals to all worlds are thrown open and you can freely enter them. This is a very potent time for any magick making because the portals are open and communication with Divine energies is particularly strong.

The element of water has long been regarded as a source of life, mystery, and power. Throughout history, cultures and traditions worldwide have honoured deities associated with the water element, each embodying various aspects of this mysterious and ever-changing element.

The most famous probably deity of water is - of course- the God of the Seas, Poseidon. As one of the twelve Olympian gods, Poseidon holds tremendous power and influence over the natural world. He is often depicted wielding a mighty trident, with which he can create storms, earthquakes, and tidal waves. Sailors and fishermen often invoked Poseidon's protection before embarking on voyages, seeking his blessing for safe travels and plentiful catches. Various festivals and rituals were held in his honour in Greece during the ancient times, celebrating his dominion over the sea.

In Roman mythology, Neptune is the counterpart of the Greek Neptune. As the god of water and the sea, Neptune is similarly associated with the mighty and very unpredictable nature of the sea. Neptune is often depicted riding a chariot drawn by sea horses, a symbol of his dominance over the seas.

While Neptune shares many characteristics with the Greek Poseidon, his significance in Roman culture was slightly different. Ancient Romans worshipped Neptune as the god of freshwater springs, such as wells and springs, in addition to his role as god of the sea. Gradually, as Roman maritime activities expanded, Neptune's association with the sea became more prominent.

The Aztec mythology also has two Water deities: Chalchiuhtlique and Tlaloc.

Chalchiuhtlique, known as the goddess of horizontal waters, is believed to rule over all bodies of water, including rivers, lakes, and oceans, and she symbolizes renewal, abundance and fertility. Chalchiuhtlique is often depicted with blue skin and hollow eyes that reflect the depths of the waters she rules.
As a goddess of fertility and abundance, Chalchiuhtlique was honoured in rituals that aimed to ensure the society's prosperity and the success of the harvest season. Her worshipers often performed rituals that involved hopping like frogs in water, a practice believed to win the goddess's favour and promote fertility.

Nereid half reclining on the back of a seahorse, fresco from Pompeii, Public Domain

The other Aztec god, Tlaloc, was the supreme god of rain and storms. He was very important god in Aztec mythology. He is often described as the husband of Chalchiuhtlique. He was feared unleash destructive floods. He was worshipped for his ability though to control waters and bring the life- giving rain. His appareance was fearsome, with large, round eyes and fangs protruding from his mouth. As the god of rain, Tlaloc was honoured with human sacrifices, including the drowning of children, to appease him and ensure favourable weather for agriculture. He also had a prominent place in the Aztec pantheon, with temples dedicated to his worship.

Lastly, it is worth mentioning the Canaanite god, Yam, the god of Sea and Chaos. He embodies the primordial and destructive forces of the sea and is often associated with storms and floods. In Canaanite myths, Yam is depicted as a fierce deity and his turbulent nature of Yam reflects the catastrophic force of the sea. He is sometimes associated with sea monsters or other serpentine creatures. In a cosmic battle, Yam is defeated by the storm god Baal, who represents order and fertility. The struggle between Yam and Baal symbolizes the eternal conflict between chaos and order, a theme that dominates many mythological traditions.

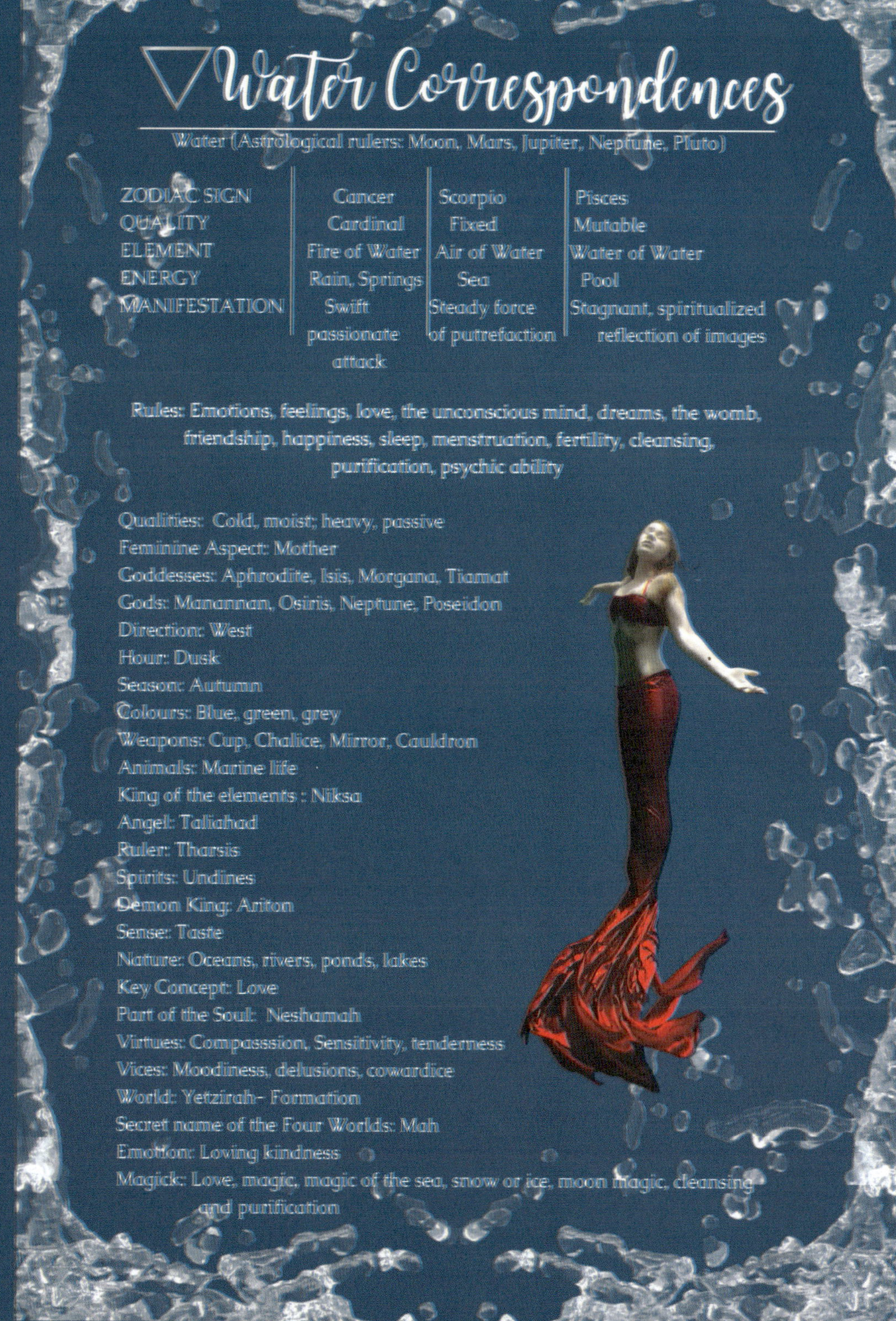

▽Water Correspondences

Water (Astrological rulers: Moon, Mars, Jupiter, Neptune, Pluto)

ZODIAC SIGN	Cancer	Scorpio	Pisces
QUALITY	Cardinal	Fixed	Mutable
ELEMENT	Fire of Water	Air of Water	Water of Water
ENERGY	Rain, Springs	Sea	Pool
MANIFESTATION	Swift passionate attack	Steady force of putrefaction	Stagnant, spiritualized reflection of images

Rules: Emotions, feelings, love, the unconscious mind, dreams, the womb, friendship, happiness, sleep, menstruation, fertility, cleansing, purification, psychic ability

Qualities: Cold, moist; heavy, passive
Feminine Aspect: Mother
Goddesses: Aphrodite, Isis, Morgana, Tiamat
Gods: Manannan, Osiris, Neptune, Poseidon
Direction: West
Hour: Dusk
Season: Autumn
Colours: Blue, green, grey
Weapons: Cup, Chalice, Mirror, Cauldron
Animals: Marine life
King of the elements : Niksa
Angel: Taliahad
Ruler: Tharsis
Spirits: Undines
Demon King: Ariton
Sense: Taste
Nature: Oceans, rivers, ponds, lakes
Key Concept: Love
Part of the Soul: Neshamah
Virtues: Compasssion, Sensitivity, tenderness
Vices: Moodiness, delusions, cowardice
World: Yetzirah- Formation
Secret name of the Four Worlds: Mah
Emotion: Loving kindness
Magick: Love, magic, magic of the sea, snow or ice, moon magic, cleansing and purification

In myths, water is associated with undines. Undines are elemental beings stemming from the writings of Paracelsus. The term Undine comes from the Latin unda, meaning "wave". Undines symbolism is the personification and spiritual manifestation of water. The origins of Undines can be traced back to ancient Greek mythology, which cites a group of sea nymphs called Oceanides. Oceanides would assist seafaring men in navigation when lost and provide safe passage to the ships. In European lore, Undine meaning dealt with the wandering spirits of love-lorn women. Tales indicate these female spirits are enchantingly beautiful and relatively benign, but like any god or spirit, they've got a temper when crossed. The undines spiritual meaning it would be to remain honest, open, and transparent in all your dealings in life.

THE ANCIENT ASCLEPIEIA

HEALING AND DREAM

by Yiannis Kokkinos

Asclepius

Asclepius, according to the ancient Greek poet Hesiod, was the son of the god Apollo and the mortal Coronida. In other words, he was a demigod. He possessed excellent skills as a doctor and healer, which he acquired next to the wise centaur Chiron, who raised him on the sacred mountain of Pelion. He had such a great reputation that the king of Crete, Minos, sent him his dead son, Glaucus, to bring him back to life. One day as Asclepius was contemplating how to bring him back to life, a snake began to coil and climb up the rod on which he was leaning. Asclepius, frightened, struck and killed the serpent. Then he was astonished to see the following scene. Another snake approached the slain serpent, bit it, and resurrected it! Asclepius understood that this was Nature's way of giving him the answer: the snake's venom. He immediately took the venom and made it into medicine. With it, he prepared a substance, which he gave to the dead Glaucus and raised him from the dead. Since then the snake became the companion of Asclepius and became established as a symbol of medicine and pharmacology.

The gods, however, never forgave Asclepius for his success in finding the medicine to raise the dead. It was an unacceptable thing to do because it disturbed the natural order of things. They felt that by doing so, men would no longer be mortal, and therefore they would lose a great advantage they had over them, immortality. Therefore Zeus thunderbolt Asclepius, who subsequently evolved into a higher god and in this capacity would be worshipped by humans.

The healing temples

The temples of Asclepius, which were healing centres of antiquity, flourished around the 7th to the 4th century BC. There were about one hundred and seventy of them, scattered all over the territory of Hellenism at that time: in Attica, the Peloponnese, Western Greece, the Aegean islands, Crete, Asia Minor, as far away as Cilicia, Rome, and Cyrene in Africa. In the Asclepieia, apart from the hero, sacred physician, and healer Asclepius, were worshipped in parallel, and occasionally his father Apollo, his mythological children Hygeia, Panacea, Telesphoros, Iasus, etc. as well as, his supposed children, Machaon and Podaleirius. These according to Homer were doctors and took part in the Trojan War.

The largest and most famous Asclepieion was at Epidaurus. The well-known ancient theatre with its excellent acoustics built there and still in operation today was a part of the healing centre's facilities. Devotees and supplicants without any social or economic distinction went to the temple of Epidaurus to be cured of health problems. But they had to follow a strict preparation process. First, the pilgrim supplicant (patient) entering from the porticoes followed the Sacred Way leading to the temple of Asclepius. After the temple, the supplicant had to stand at the Holy Fountain, the water of which was used for the purification of the body and symbolic mental purification. This washing and cleansing with water had a huge symbolic significance and we find it in all the important temples in the healing centres and oracles of antiquity. The pilgrim then went to the altar to offer a sacrifice of an animal, usually a bull. After the sacrifice, they would pass into the sanctuary where they would see the offerings and inscriptions of those who had been healed. After the prayers, purifications, and sacrifices, the supplicant had to go through religious tests to strengthen their faith so that their soul would be ready to come into contact with the Divine.

The priests who guided the devotees had to create intense self-submission and religious excitement so that God would appear in their sleep, while the devotion was emphasized with hymns. The preparation included special diets, fasting, baths, attending theatrical and musical performances, reading, exercise, massage, inhalation of fumes (probably with the use of psychotropic substances), and discussions with the priests and doctors of the Asclepieion. After the prayers, purifications, and sacrifices, the supplicant had to undergo religious tests to strengthen his faith and prepare his soul for the encounter with God. The use of running water was very basic, and the patients also drank tea made from various herbs and other medicinal mixtures, which were thought to have a healing but mainly sedative effect - which, as we have said, may have contained psychotropic substances. In fact, sometimes the sick person got well at this stage, without the need to continue any further.
The process culminated in Enkoimesis or incubation. A dream-like state, something between anaesthesia and hypnosis. The priests would lead the sick person to the Sanctuary (or Sanctus or Enkomiser), where the devotee, lying on an animal skin, would wait to see the god in a dream to guide them through the cure. Asclepius appeared in dreams as a bearded man holding a rod, or as a man's hand touching the affected part. Healing dreams with snakes were also common, and good omens of healing were the appearance of a dog - considered a companion of Asclepius- or a cock, also a symbol of the god. The next day, patients would describe what they had seen in their dreams to the priests, and depending on the dream or the progress of the Enkoimesis, if they had not already been cured, they would be given a treatment to follow. Finally, the whole record of the illness, dream, and cure was recorded on tablets and displayed in public view.

Gods and people

In general, the ancient Greeks believed in the epiphanies of the gods. The appearances of Asclepius back then occurred in a world that believed in such phenomena. In dreams, the soul came into contact with those divine forces surrounding people and the world, which it could not conceive when awakened. But there is a question. How could people who had dreams get well because of what appeared in their dreams? Because if we accept that the God did not exist and therefore did not act, that leaves only the preparatory treatment and the dreams themselves with the healing that occurred either directly during the dreams or later through some medical treatment resulting from their content.

The fact that people who went to the Asclepieia were having dreams is understandable. Everyone went with that purpose in mind, while some who failed to dream were in the minority. It is equally understandable that the subject of their dreams would be Asclepius and their illnesses because that is what they desired, and it is understandable that they would see the god helping them or advising them in the form he was represented on his statues because that is how he was imprinted on them. They came to seek god's help feeling excited after a long arduous journey made solely for this purpose, being concerned and worried about their sickness and suffering. They saw the imposing sanctuary of God, stayed there for several days, took part in mystical rituals, came into contact with other patients and venerable priests, and read the tablets on which were written dozens of successful cures and thanksgivings. After all this, how could they not dream in the way they did? It is no exaggeration to say that in a world where the gods were still alive, anyone who visited a temple and expected a divine vision was sure to have such dreams. So in this particular case, these visions were completely normal and expected.

The priests would lead the sick person to the Sanctuary (or Sanctus or Enkomiser), where the devotee, lying on an animal skin, would wait to see the god in a dream to guide them through the cure.

A contemporary point of view

The dreams, then, that people in the Asclepieia claimed to have had - and undoubtedly did have - are easy to understand, despite their metaphysical content. But why did the patients get well if they were only dreaming? How could they feel immediate relief after a simple vision? How could they recover through a treatment based on general techniques and drugs in preparation for the Egkoimesis or after a fanciful interpretation of their dream images ("messages") by the priests? It is obvious that unconscious psychological processes were involved in the healings, which healed through the uplifting of the soul and through faith in the miracle that was expected to take place, regardless of whether the treatment they received from the priests was effective or not. We see such miracles occurring even today regardless of whether they are attributed to other gods, shamans, mystics, or ordinary people with deep faith and self-control.

But what is the relationship of modern medicine to the Egkoimesis and the whole process of inducing healing dreams? Experts now admit that most diseases have serious psychosomatic dimensions. Today's advances in neuroscience have revealed what we have always suspected but could not prove: that any method which induces spiritual uplift has a therapeutic effect. But the place where the dream has a leading role is in psychoanalysis, in which, according to Sigmund Freud, it is the channel of communication with the human unconscious. Through dreams, we receive camouflaged information and messages from the depths of our soul that are extremely difficult to retrieve in any other way. If we assume that somehow the soul "knows" what is good and what is not good for us, it is certain that it will not only try to protect us from anything painful and harmful, but it will also give us the solution we need to overcome it.

Here let us not forget that not all patients were admitted to the Asclepieia. Those suffering from severe and incurable diseases were considered to have been punished by the Gods for some reason, so no other God or man had the right to intervene and heal them - only to relieve the sufferer of the symptoms. Religion and healing were inextricably linked in pre-Hippocratic times (before 400 BC) and the exclusive privilege of priests or their disciples. So we cannot know with certainty whether this concept was a tactical move by the priesthood to avoid having its effectiveness challenged or whether they did indeed consider any human intervention against the divine will as hubris [contempt] that brought punishment. So in the Asclepieia the relatively milder problems were selected and treated, which to the eyes of the ordinary people might seem very serious but to the doctors - priests were familiar and amenable to treatment.

Dreams therapeutic contribution would be formally reintroduced two and a half millennia later by Freud as a key element of psychoanalysis.

Antiquity and now

By collecting the methods, rituals, and means (substances) used by the Ancients in the process of Enlightenment we can easily see similarities with many methods of healing which today are described as alternatives but then they were practiced as the main ones, without knowing anything other than their effectiveness. So we can see that massages were performed, i.e. an early reflexology, maybe even reiki, herbal therapy, maybe even homeopathy, flower remedies and herb essential oils, music therapy - dance therapy, physiotherapy - pilates, hypnotherapy, and probably also thermal baths. The existence of a thermal spring in a strong energetic location was a key indicator of where an ancient sanctuary would be chosen to be built. People back then lived in total contact with nature and were very sensitive to its powers. Many of the hot springs of that time may have dried up, but even today visitors to ancient monuments can feel the positive energy that overwhelms these places all over the world, especially where Ancient Greece flourished. Focusing specifically on the dream, as we saw above its therapeutic contribution would be formally reintroduced two and a half millennia later by Freud as a key element of psychoanalysis. Along with hypnosis, they would become the first methods in modern times for entering one's unconscious. The development of the science of psychology has changed directions along the way and dreaming and hypnosis have again fallen by the wayside, but the acceptance of the existence of dark areas of the human psyche that affect one's health physically or mentally is now well-established. The Asclepieia of antiquity can be said with certainty that in their own way and knowledge, they were pioneering centres of healing not only for their time but also for the modern present.

Mengs, Helios als Personifikation des Mittags

SUMMER SOLSTICE: CURSED OR BLESSED

by Evangelia Papanikou

"The brightest sun on one side,
on the other the new moon
fade in memory like those breasts.
In between them the chasm of a starry night
life's cataclysm"

(George Seferis, "Summer Solstice",
Translation by E. Papanikou)

What could happen on the shortest night of the year? With the summer solstice experience at its peak, the earth's axis turns towards Helios, the Greek Sun god who sees everything and knows everything on earth, day and night, and burns with the truth what humanity seeks and longs for...

Hans Adam Weissenkircher - Helios on His Chariot (Detail)

Once upon an ancient time, in the night of the summer solstice, a hideous feast took place where the guest of honor was Thyestes, Atreus's own brother but also the man who had an affair with Atreus' wife. Atreus decided to punish Thyestes in a manner reminiscent of their grandfather Tantalus who had served up his own son and brought a curse down upon the family line. He invited his brother Thyestes to a special banquet, having him think that their reigning differences were over, where he arranged that body parts of Thyestes' sons were served up as the main course. Thyestes only realised the horrible truth after consumption when Atreus produced resentfully the toes and fingers of his murdered sons in vengeance. In sheer disgust, shock and absolute sickness Thyestes cursed deeply Atreus' family line in specific, resulting in a curse that Atreus' sons carried to their horrible deaths after an equally disturbed life.

Aegisthus was Thyestes' son by his own daughter Pelopia. He was conceived by Pelopia's rape in the hopes that the oracle Thyestes had received would be realised and thus, his own son and grandson at the same time would be the chosen one to take revenge. A subsequent summer solstice night, Aegisthus was born and through a weird line of events, on another summer solstice, he indeed murdered Atreus, the man who had actually raised him in a twist of fate as his third son, next to Agamemnon and Menelaus, as Aegisthus was abandoned by his own mother when she realised that her father raped her but he was rescued by the palace. Atreus' murder was not enough, however, to lift the curse on his family line.

It was in the night of an ancient summer solstice, deep in the forest, when Orpheus was dismembered alive by the Maenads, just like Dionysus Zagreas once and for ever was and consumed by them to keep him for ever inside them. Ritualistically, initiatory and mysteriously, initially and periodically in order for both of them to rise again and exist forever, in light and dark, intertwined in a vortex of art and religion.

Hercules never died but was deified through his purification of the magic flames of a fire lit under the night sky of a summer solstice.

In modern times, the ancient customs of the nights of the summer solstice are still curiously preserved. Ceremonies of purifying and occult character still take place in the country side and the city corner's at the same cosmic time joining the male and female divine.

In Greek folklore single women carry water to their home, in pitchers, from a spring or a well or a river, immediately after the sunrise. This water is called "unspoken" or "silent" because the women should not talk or laugh at all while transporting it, even if boys or men try to provoke them on purpose.

Late in the night, with well-hidden their wishes and their secret thoughts, those men who participate in such folklore customs, having prepared themselves mentally, jump over the specially high lit open fires to the other side, breaking through earthly stereotypes and barriers, traveling through the mystic collective subconscious.

Eventually, when everyone is in a state of trance

Midsummer Eve
Edward Robert Hughes c. 1908

Gustave Doré, "A Midsummer Night's Dream". Circa 1870

A_Midsummer_Night's_Dream_Robert_Fowler_(1853-1926)

and exhausted, when all vital questions have been answered and the light of fire has been transferred into the eyes of the present male participants, the fire is put out by the female participants, throwing at it streaks of water from their jugs, containing the same water they drank earlier. And then, when everyone's eyes are filled with the form of their desire, rapt in the flashes of flame, they dream and guess answers to secret looks and trite questions.

Those who succeed will get an answer to a secret question about their own future or other rewards, such as good fortune and various strengths and abilities, as per the variations of the legend.

Be careful the night of the summer solstice, not to be looked at, not to be talked at, not to be desired. Do not jump fires. Do not fall in love or do not have someone fall in love with you, because during a ritual with a primal, magical or religious content, when the gazes mystically cloud or clear, the spoken or implied words could come true. You have been warned...

No matter how great the chasm and cataclysmic terror of life may be, mythology continues to be a haven of the human consciousness, not only for the primitive human beings, but also for the Homo Sapiens, beyond science and closer to our inner core truth...

Or has any of this not happened? Lest you think that it is only orgy and hierogamy rituals taking place in the summer solstice... There is so much more possible, from absolute dark to absolute bright light and explosive energy with a deeper connection at the unexplored depths of the mind and soul, without horrible curses and hexes but with binding spells and natural enchantments.

Blessed, timeless and mythical summer solstice!

THE UNSPOKEN WATER

In Greek folklore, the term unspoken water is the water that is collected and carried by young girls (usually unmarried), for the execution of the so-called divination custom of "Klidonas". It was a very important magical ingredient. Specifically, the unspoken water is transported by pitchers from a spring or well or river, on the night of the eve of the celebration of the birth of St. John the Baptist on June 24, and immediately after sunset. It is named unspoken because during its carrying the girls should remain completely silent against any jokes, teasing, provocations, or even intimidation if they suffer from the boys who come their way specifically for this purpose.

Another version of the folklore is that the unspoken water was collected late at night, the first night of the New Year. However, someone could collect it any time during the year, but that day it was more powerful. Next to the spring, the girls were leaving behind a handful of sugar for the three Moires (Fates).

The lore says that that night the Moires were coming out to distribute the fortunes to people. Moires were sitting next to the spring to get some rest, wash or drink water. Therefore, the sugar was a treat to them, a way the girls made sure that their fortune was going to be 'sweet' throughout the year.

In Scotland, there is a similar custom, about the unspoken water. It was believed to have healing properties and based on the Etymological Dictionary of the Scottish Language, it was supposed to be collected "from under a bridge, over which the living pass and the dead are carried, brought in the dawn or twilight to the house of a sick person, without the bearer's speaking, either in going or returning".
On The Mirror of Literature, Amusement, and Instruction, of 1828, we read that the "modes of application are various: sometimes the invalid takes three draughts of it before anything is spoken. Sometimes it is thrown over the houses, the vessel in which it was contained being thrown after it". It is believed that the custom is long obsolete.

Danaides-
John William Waterhouse

ALINA VON

KEIPIGRAFIE

Immerse yourself in Alina's magical world!

Interview to Anastasia Diakidi

Model: Moonlight Dragonfly

Model: Moonlight Dragonfly

Hello Alina, thank you so much for being here. We welcome you to Imaginarium World. So please, tell us a little about you how did you start your journey into Photography?

Hello, thank you for having me here. So my name is Alina, I am 25 years young and a professional photographer. Also I am a make-up artist, dressmaker, mum, artist and businesswoman. Originally from Saarland, I now live in the Palatinate with my long-term partner Jonas and our daughter. My path began when I stood in front of the camera for the first time at the age of 16. Until I was 21 years old, I was exclusively a model. Then I needed some distance due to bad experiences, but after a few months, I realized "There is something missing" and bought a cheap SLR from the year 2004 at that time for little money. That was the start. Even as a child, I always wanted to be my own boss. In 2019, I finally fulfilled this long-held dream.

Back then, I would never have dared to dream that my schedule would one day be full of shoots or that my pictures would be featured in trade magazines.

Starting with classic portrait photography, I now mainly work in the cosplay and staged photography segment, but weddings, reportages, baby bump and family shoots are also subjects that are close to my heart. As a mum of a little daughter, I know only too well the need to have pictures of the children.

What does inspire you to create a project?

My grandfather had always told me self-made-up fairy tales from his heart. He is my greatest source of inspiration to this day; from him I have also inherited many fairy tale books that have already a few decades old. Of course, authors like Tolkien, Brent Weeks, and G.R.R. Martin are not to be missed. Their worlds also inspired me to dive into my own world. 15 years ago I discovered RPG for myself - D&D just for writing. So some of my characters exist a bit longer and currently, I have already created four of my own characters.
In the pictures you can see - Galewan, my dragon shifter (red hair, white-golden scales), and Tyditea, my nymph (red hair, green dress).
The worlds I play with my RP friends are vivid, realistic in a fantasy style, and invite you to linger. Here goes a big thanks to one of my biggest sources of inspiration - My "Saga Family".

Model: Moonlight Dragonfly

Model: Moonlight Dragonfly

Why portraits?

The beauty of people is worth capturing. And if you can then turn them into mythical creatures, that's priceless to me.

Have you or your work been affected by the pandemic and how did you overcome the obstacles? Do you find that the pandemic changed your art and the way you had to work?

In fact, the Corona time was not very critical for me. Since I became a mother two months before the outbreak of the pandemic, the year 2020 was otherwise planned for me anyway. And when we were allowed to work again as photographers in Germany in 2021, I implemented the creativity from 2020 directly - my first event with another photographer arose, and two months later my own dragon event! So the pandemic actually had only advantages for me.

How would you describe your Art?

I asked my followers because I just can't answer this question. And the answers were:
Magical, Mystical, and Dreamy.

Nowadays that pretty much everyone has a camera, what defines the real Photographer?

In that sense, I am not a "real" photographer. I have not done any apprenticeship in the profession. But I have always been very creative and also self-taught. Therefore, I would say: the eye and the stamina. Why the stamina? Because it is very difficult to get a foothold in the market and find your place.

Are you only a photographer at work or do you use your camera in your everyday life?

In everyday life, I use my cell phone most of the time. When I go with the family to an event, the camera is also sometimes there to capture the moments. But mainly I really use it to create fantasy worlds.

Find out [illegible]
Instagram [illegible]

Model: Moonlight Dragonfly

Where is Magic in life?

In your heart, for sure.

Do you work with clients for commissions or only with professional models?

I am a bookable photographer, but I also work TFP basis - not even with professional models. Most of my "girls" - so I call them - are just like me, just creative minds who love to escape everyday life. Of course, long friendships have already developed here. But there are also initial customers who are now among my girls. It is important to me that the vibe is right and that you are on the same wavelength in a collaboration. Of course, the fun should not come too short.

Tell us about your plans for the near future.

In June I'm giving my workshop in cosplay photography for photographers- planning is in full swing and I'm super excited! You always doubt something about yourself and whether you are made for it at all. But without trying it, you can not find out if it is something for you.

Next spring I organize my first con/fair. It will be a big fantasy event, which will go over a weekend long. Together with my partner, the Rosengarten Zweibrücken - the oldest rose garden in Europe, I will realize this event. There will be six different theme worlds and it should stand out. Only individual craftsmen will be invited to show their work, there will be walking acts, and the theme worlds will each be set up like a big shooting set - so that it will hopefully be a magnet for photographers, models, and interested people. I am currently putting a lot of heart and soul into the theme and backdrop construction is the be-all and end-all at home right now.

FOR MORE CHECK:
keipigrafie.de

& Instagram:
@keipigrafie

Model: Alina

The Flying Dutch (Wo)man

Marije van der Ende is a Dutch singer, living in Germany. Next to her work as a singer and singing teacher, she makes fantasy and historical costumes and does photography under the name: The Flying Dutch(wo)man. Everything from extravagant rococo dresses, and colourful flower fairy costumes, to mermaid crowns and elven outfits. As long as it transports you to a different time and place, Marije is up for it. She also tries to capture this in her photography work, dressing people in her handmade costumes, and styling them accordingly.
Marije also takes romantic self-portraits using a tripod and remote control.
Fin out more about this talented artist on
Instagram: https://instagram.com/theflyingdutchwoman
&
Facebook: https://www.facebook.com/theflyingdutchwomanEU

Inside a Fairytale

Step into a World of Self-Discovery.

Inside a Fairytale is a platform that invites you to immerse yourself in a world of wonder and fantasy. This new entertaining platform offers an immersive audio experience that combines enchanting stories, original orchestral music, and inspiring messages to transport you to a realm of magic and adventure. Inside A Fairytale is the perfect escape for anyone seeking a magical adventure.

Inside a Fairytale is the passion project of Maria Rogers, a classical pianist, singer-songwriter, and lover of all things fantastical. With a BA degree in Music and Theatre and multiple awards gained throughout her music career, Maria has poured her heart and soul into this project.

The platform features three categories: Immersive Stories, Fantasy Music, and Secret Messages. Each category offers a different experience to delight and inspire visitors of the website.

Immersive Stories takes you on a journey through a world of enchantment, with each story crafted by Maria from scratch. With richly detailed descriptions and captivating plotlines, these stories transport you to a world of magic and wonder.

Fantasy Music offers a collection of original compositions created specifically for Inside a Fairytale. Each track is an evocative soundscape that will transport you to a different realm.

Secret Messages offers a collection of inspiring

Photo Canva stock

Experience the magic within you and find answers to life's biggest questions.

quotes and phrases that will uplift and motivate you. These messages are handpicked by Maria and are perfect for anyone in need of a little inspiration and encouragement.

Inside a Fairytale offers a unique listening experience that can be enjoyed anywhere, anytime. All the stories are also child friendly, so the platform can be enjoyed by the whole family and it's completely free!

By exploring what Inside a Fairytale has to offer, not only will you develop a deeper understanding of yourself, but you will also learn to trust your intuition, increase your creativity and gain a sense of purpose and direction in your life. You will have the tools to unlock your inner wisdom, and live more authentically and in tune with yourself.

The carefully crafted stories, music, and messages will take you on a journey to connect with your inner light, joy, energy, and life force.

Please check this wonderful and free platform and let yourself to be carried away in magical lands.

For more information and details, please visit https://insideafairytale.co.uk or contact Maria at welcome[at]insideafairytale.co.uk

The Witch's Cabinet

Beauty and Wellbeing with the Guidance of the Moon

**All the planetary aspects the Moon forms are calculated for 9a.m UTC.*

By Lucinda

Dear magical friends,

The month of June begins with the Moon in the sign of Scorpio and on the 2nd of June, it will oppose Uranus. If you can not sleep make a drink

from a teaspoon of valerian, a passionflower, and a linden. Pour the mixture into two cups of hot water, leave for 5 minutes, and strain. Drink one cup in the afternoon and one before bed.

On June 3, the Moon moves into Sagittarius. Do some exercise or take a long walk. If you are into adventure, take advantage of it for more demanding sports and activities but be careful later on during the day as the Moon squares Saturn and this could indicate a small accident or backache. Do not overdo it.

On June 4, we have a Full Moon in the Gemini-Sagittarius axis. The so-called Full Moon of Christ or Gemini. It is the moment we celebrate the Festival of Humanity. The Festival of Humanity is one of the three great spiritual festivals. During this, you celebrate the goodwill of humanity and for this it is also called the Festival of Good Will. It's the moment we celebrate our natural inclination to unity. People from all over the world pray and meditate for the good of humanity. They express an invocation to light, love, and goodness.
So on the 4th of the month, take some time to pray for humanity. You will be attuned to souls around the world who pray for the virtues taught by great spiritual teachers, like Christ and Buddha.

Here is the Great Invocation, a prayer for all people:

From the point of Light within the Mind of God

Let light stream forth into the minds of men

Let Light descend on Earth.

From the point of Love within the Heart of God

Let love stream forth into the hearts of men
May Christ return to Earth.

From the Centre where the Will of God is known

Let purpose guide the little wills of men
The purpose which the Masters know and serve

From the Centre which we call the race of men

Let the Plan of Love and Light work out
And may it seal the door where evil dwells

Let Light and Love and Power restore the Plan on Earth.

On June 6 with Moon in Capricorn is a good day to work with the earth or do some woodwork. If you have wooden floors or furniture, you can polish or repair them until the 8th of the month.

Photo Canva stock

On June 8, with the Moon in Aquarius, if you have cramps,

massage with 15 ml of almond oil,
3 drops of marjoram essential oil,
2 drops of chamomile essential oil,
and 2 drops of mandarin essential oil.

On **June 11, the Moon is in Pisces and there it will meet Neptune.** A day when we can be hypersensitive. Let us leave the demanding work for later, and let us spend our day at sea. If you do not like or can not plan to go to the beach, it is a good day to meditate. Visualize whatever weighs you down, goes away. Take a bath or a shower and feel the energy of the water in your body cleansing you.

On the 12th of June with Moon in Aries, do house cleaning with lye.

We can very easily make homemade lye and store it in the refrigerator for a long time.
We will need:

6 cups of water - we can also use rainwater
2 tablespoons ash (clean, not burnt plastics and other chemicals and well sifted)
If we need a larger amount we increase the doses.

The procedure is very simple: Boil the water and add the ashes. Stir for a while and let it boil for 5 minutes. Remove from the heat and let the ashes settle. Once this is done, strain it and put it in the fridge. It can be used immediately after its preparation.

Lye has many uses in cleaning, gardening, confectionery, and of course hygiene and hair and skincare.

On the June 14 the Moon in Taurus conjuncts Jupiter. This is a pleasant and protective meeting between the two celestial bodies.

The day the Moon and Jupiter create an energy shield is a good day to do the same with your body.

4 tablespoons rosemary
2 tablespoons lavender
1 tablespoon juniper seeds
4 bay leaves
1 tablespoon salt

Put the solid materials in white tulle and tie it well. Dip the pouch in the hot water bath and let it cool down. Soak and let the herbs absorb negative energy.

On June 18, we have a New Moon in Gemini. Many of you are either leaving for a vacation soon or you are planning your summer excursions.

I would like to share with you a nice protection spell for the holidays. An amulet that you will have with you when you leave home.

You will need

1 stone of aventurine
1 stone of turquoise
1 moonstone
3 drops of sandalwood essential oil
3 drops of cedar essential oil
and a small cloth bag.

The night before you leave the house put aventurine on the north side of the house, turquoise on the east side of the house, moonstone on the south side of the house. Drop on each stone and a drop of each oil.

In the morning, collect the crystals that have been activated based on Feng shui and the power of the moon. Put them in the bag while you say the following words: "Thank you Moon for safe travel and make my home and my family happy too". Take your stone bag with you to be protected on your travels.

On **June 19, the Moon is, in its house of rulership, in Cancer.** It is a nice day for kneading bread. Try experimenting with bread as there are many types of flour now on the market to create wonderful loaves of bread. I especially love bread with honey so I would suggest you add a little honey and cinnamon to your recipe. If you have children they will love it.

On **June 21, we have the Summer Solstice**. The day is a celebration as the Sun reaches the highest point of its journey. Even the Moon celebrates the Sun this year,, as **Moon is in Leo**, the sign the Sun rules. Today is the longest day and that is why it has been associated with expansion and greater energy. If you want you can do a summer meditation on the day of the summer solstice. I would suggest you meditate somewhere out, in nature, if your schedule permits it. In your meditation, feel the energy of the earth that nourishes the soil. Listen to the soil and its growth, imagine the branches and roots of the trees as a huge network that embraces the earth and through the water the nutrients travel and give life; feel this vitality, the growth and the opening of life and the flow of creation. Lie on the ground and feel the life around you.

The ancient Saxon tradition of the *fire of necessity or fire of need*, involved building a huge bonfire that was ignited by friction, never by fuel or sparks from an existing fire. The flames were thought to ward off evil spirits; the higher the flames, the farther away the evil was warded. Any food cooked over this bonfire was believed to have special healing properties.

To evoke the feeling of the fire of need, you may find it desirable to burn candles for three consecutive days. Choose a candle that has an adequate life span. If you cannot find such candles, you can use three twenty-four-hour candles, lighting them in succession.

Choose bright, warm colours for the Sun. Carve an equilateral cross within a circle on the side of the candle with rays extending outward to pay homage to this peak moment of the dominant light.

Keep the lit candle in an undisturbed place. When you need to leave your altar, leave the candles burning in the middle of the tub. If you are using shorter-lived candles, remember to light the next one after the first, and so on, before the candle burns out completely.

On **June 24** it is the traditional feast of the Midsummer and is combined with the feast of St. John the Baptist. In addition to the various celebrations and customs that exist today for the sun, there are many customs associated with the birthday of John the Baptist.

One of them is the ancient custom of Klidonas, celebrated in Greece. Klidonas is a divination process one of the most ritual-related traditions of Greece, according to which unmarried girls could reveal the identity of their future husband. On the eve of St. John's, the unmarried girls gather in one of the houses of the village and some of them are instructed to bring the Unspoken Water from the well or the spring. When returning home, the water must be put in a clay container in which the girls put inside a personal object. The vessel is then covered with a red cloth which is tied tightly with a string and asks for the help of Saint John in the prophecy. The container remains in the open air all night, under the light of the stars. It is said that women will dream of their future husband that night. On the day of Agianni (St. John's), before the sun rises so as not to neutralize the magical influence of the stars, or alternatively in some areas, at twelve o'clock in the afternoon, when the sun "trembles"; the women gather again, this time to open the clay pot. They take the object they have thrown in and with songs that are recited randomly try to connect the message of the lyrics with the future of each girl.

In Kefalonia of Greece, they poured melted lead into the unspoken water and just as the lead pours into the container and into the cold water, it cools immediately and forms various shapes. The older one and the wiser studied the shapes and gave oracles. At dusk when the divination process ended, each girl filled her mouth with a sip of unspoken water and stood in front of an open window until she heard the first male name; that would be the name of the man she would marry.

Nowadays, the custom of Klidonas is no longer performed in the cities. However, if you have a spring, a river or lake that you can visit in the park, collect some Unspoken Water and either perform a ritual of your choice or just keep it as a magical ingredient. You can also pour a little water on the four corners of the house for blessing.

Also if you have fields or woods near you and you know a good deal about foraging, it is a good day to go out to collect the St. Johns Wort, which is also a very good weed for protection.

On the 27th of the month with the Moon in Libra and in a sextile with Venus and Mars, take advantage of the day to achieve significant extensions in matters of relationships, home, or even social contacts. A good day to spend with your friends and loved ones, while you can also deal with the renovation of the house. Do a good vent to let the negative energy go and let the optimism and joy come in.

On **July 2nd, Moon is in Sagittarius and forms a trine with Mars**. This is a day that favours physical activity, sports and fun. Great time to join a fitness group or go for a run.

On **July 3rd a Full Moon in the Cancer/Capricorn axis takes place while forming a favourable trine with Jupiter.**

Reflect on the past, as Cancer and Capricorn are signs related to nostalgia and family. Call an old friend or family member that you haven't spoken to in a while and reminisce.

This is also an ideal time to connect with nature. Take a long walk outside, tend to your garden, or breathe in fresh air.

On July 6, the Moon is in the sign of Aquarius. This is a good day to make a cream for varicose veins.

Melt in a baking pan butter with chopped agrimony leaves. Filter it and store it in jars; it is works wonders for varicose veins.

On **July 11, Moon is in Taurus and during the day forms a sextile with Saturn and a conjunction with Jupiter.** A good time to deal with whatever you want to have a long-lasting effect.

A mantra that you could work on these days is:

"My god,
Give me the peace to accept the things I cannot change,
The courage to change what I can,
And the Wisdom to know the difference"

On **July 13, with the Moon in Gemini**, make a body exfoliating cream.

Mix 1 cup of virgin olive oil with 2 cups of sea salt. Add a few drops of peppermint essential oil. Rub the mixture all over the body. Then rinse with the shower.

On July 17, the New Moon is taking place on the sign of Cancer.

The New Moon in Cancer is an auspicious time to focus on our emotions and connections to our home, family, and loved ones. Cancer is a water sign, and the Moon is especially strong in its ruling sign. This makes the New Moon a time to focus on our inner world, emotions, and relationships. Set aside a quiet, peaceful space in your home where you can perform your ritual. Light candles, burn incense or sage and play soft music to create a soothing atmosphere. Take some time to journal about your emotions and any unresolved issues or concerns that have been on your mind. This can help you release any negative energy and clear your mind for setting intentions. Afterwards, set intentions around creating a peaceful, harmonious home environment, improving relationships with loved ones, and nurturing your emotional connections. Visualize your intentions in detail and focus on the emotions you want to feel as you manifest them.

You could take a bath with sea salt or essential oils to cleanse and release negative energy, or perform a ritual of pouring water over your hands, symbolizing the release of old emotions.

Alternatively, you could light a silver candle in honour of the Moon, meditate on its energy, and visualize the manifestation of your intentions.

On the 20th, the Moon will be in the sign of Leo forming a conjunction with Venus. With this aspect and placement is the right time to get your hair cut if you want it to grow stronger.

If you want you can also massage the hair and head with 50 gr. rosemary flowers and leaves in a litre of water. Boil and let cool. Apply and massage. Leave for half an hour.

The benefits of rosemary are innumerable. It has been used since antiquity because it has a high content of nutrients and antioxidants.
Rosemary helps with the problem of hair loss while enhancing the shine of the hair. Hair gets more volume as it is rich in vitamins B and C. It also activates the moisture and nutrition of the hair follicles, increasing blood circulation in the area. Reduces the appearance of grey hair, fights dandruff and greasiness. Finally, rosemary is a natural conditioner that makes hair silky and hydrated. You can only benefit from its systematic use.

On July 21, the Moon passes in Virgo and forms a trine with Jupiter.
The next two days meditate on the phrase:

"Only with the help of the heart I open my mind and truly know the depth of things."

On **July 25, the Moon is in Libra**. If you have kidney sensitivities or kidney stones, eat strawberries and drink a decoction of strawberry roots.

Boil 15 grams. roots in 3 glasses of water and drink three times a day.

On July 27, with Moon in Scorpio, if you have no sexual drive due to stress is the right time to start the Bach flower remedy of white chestnut.
This particular flower remedy is also extremely beneficial for those who suffer from dark thoughts, fear, and are unable to think clearly.

On July 30, the Moon passes in the sign of Capricorn. This is a good time for a good facial cleansing.

Make a peeling with sugar and honey, apply, and make circular motions. Rinse with warm water.
Alternatively, the recipe can be made with oil and salt.
Peeling removes toxins, dead cells, and impurities from the face and cleanses the pores.

Have a lovely magical time and a blessed Midsummer!

Lucinda

Photo Canva database

PLANETARIUM

The Diary of Planetary Influences

By Anastasia Diakidi

The dates given are when the aspects become exact. However, they start with their influence 1-2 days before and -in some cases- last 1-2 days after the given date. The degrees given mean that those who have planets or Ascendant/Midheaven on those degrees are influenced by the aspect. To get a copy of your natal chart check astro.com or email imaginarium.magazine.13@gmail.com

Cardinal Signs: Aries, Cancer, Libra, Capricorn
Fixed Signs: Taurus, Leo, Scorpio, Aquarius
Mutable Signs: Gemini, Virgo, Sagittarius, Pisces

A sign is 30° and it consists of 3 decans. A decan is the equivalent of 10 days, as a sign corresponds to 30 days. Those born on the 1st decan are born on the first 10 days (0-9°) of their sign, on the 2nd the following 10 days (10-19°) and those on the 3rd decan are born on the last 10 days (20-29°) of their sign.

2/6 Venus trine Neptune: Sensitivity and taste in love and art. Enjoyment of a fantasy. Accurate aesthetic judgments. Desire for distant things. A good day to relax with friends. It affects the Water and Earth signs or those who have planets/ASC/MC on those signs, from 25-29°.

4/6 Full Moon in Gemini: This Full Moon brings disruption and nervousness in everyday life, transport, communications, and education. There is also creativity and opportunities for establishing and spreading ideas. Beware of hasty movements and exaggeration. There will also be opportunities for relaxation.

& Mercury conjunction Uranus: The aspect has a lot of nervous tension. Appliances and machinery may break down. The mind is inventive and the aspect might help us achieve something innovative, or progressive. Technical interest and inventiveness are characteristic of this aspect. A good day to join with others for a specific cause or purpose. Bear in mind that breakups and tension are also possible, especially for the Fixed Signs. The aspect is beneficial for Cancer, Virgo, Capricorn, and Pisces. It affects the Water and Earth signs or those who have planets/ASC/MC on those signs, from 16-24°.

5/6 Venus enters Leo: This placement favours the Fire and Airs signs. Venus boosts the love life and the finances of those signs. This placement makes us seek fun and creativity within relationships. We may value more appearances. Good time for the Fire signs to make beauty/cosmetic changes.

& Venus opposition Pluto: Intense interactions with others. Financial success or achievement after great effort. New intense relationships. Sexuality. Beware of obsession, jealousy, assault, and abusive behaviours. It affects 29-30° of Cardinal Signs and those born in the first two days (0-2°) of the Fixed signs. Same degrees for those who have planets/ Ascendant/ Midheaven on those signs.

9/6 Mercury sextile Neptune: Artistic appreciation and the joys of slow living are some of the positive effects of this transit. If possible, postpone rational thinking and duties and enjoy the sea or a day in a museum. A good aspect for artists and those who were looking for inspiration and vision in their work. It affects Pisces, Taurus, Cancer, Scorpio, Virgo, and Capricorn from 25-29° and those who have planets/Ascendant in those signs and degrees.

11/6 Pluto enters Capricorn: Pluto enters Capricorn again to make the final and profound changes in the lives of those who have planets/ Ascendant/ Midheaven in the last 2 degrees of the Cardinal signs. Those changes have been initiated last December (until March) Pluto will remain in Capricorn until 20th January 2024. Plutonian events will affect also the political and economical scene of the world.

& Mercury trine Pluto: Persuasion and power in speech. A penetrating conversation might bring psychological issues to the surface. A good day for psychotherapy. The power of communication. A positive day that could potentially lead to business success from the Earth Signs, especially those who are born or have planets around 27-29°.

& Mercury enters Gemini: This placement is very good for Mercury as it is considered the sign of its rulership. This Mercury placement will improve everyone's communications. Commuting and educational changes are favourable. The Air signs will be benefited more from this placement as well as the Fire signs. Pisces, Sagittarius and Virgo may be more restless and have more mental tension.

& Venus square Jupiter: The aspect is favourable although it can be affected by excessive socializing. The desire to "party". Romantic expression has drama and exuberance. Beware of over-appreciation of something and excessive pleasures. Tendency to overeat. Beware of overspending on pleasures. Affects the Fixed signs or those with planets, Ascendant or Midheaven of 2-8° in them.

15/6 Mercury square Saturn: Limitations. Careful when driving or commuting. Unpleasant thoughts, negativity and sense of responsibility. Daily life seems heavy. It helps to organize life. Unpleasant news or heavy communication with others. Strong criticism. Affects Mutable signs or those with planets, Ascendant or Midheaven from 4-10° of these.

17/6 Mercury sextile Venus: A harmonious aspect that is beneficial for social contacts, flirting, and kind interactions. Under this influence, we are more willing to compromise and agree. A good day to appreciate the beauty and express warm feelings. Affects Air and Fire signs or those with planets, Ascendant or Midheaven of 8-14° in them.

17/6 Saturn stationary to turn retrograde: During the retrograde period, we get to experience a lot of karmic events related to our past actions. Time to reconsider our values, ethics and stability. Saturn will remain retrograde until November 10. It affects Mutable signs and those with planets, Ascendant/Midheaven in them (0-7°).

18/6 New Moon in Gemini: The New Moon in Gemini normally is a good time for communication and socializing. But this new moon forces us to pause for a moment and reconsider the structure and the moral substance and value of our ideas. There may be blockages in travel, communications and education. This is not a good time to sign contracts. Beware of hasty movements and reckless action. Reaction and stubbornness. Desire for freedom.

19/6 Sun square Neptune: Lack of clarity because unknown factors challenge the judgment. Impressionability, escapist urges, and misunderstandings. Mistakes and errors in judgment. Not a good day for business decisions or activities. Foggy or sloppy conditions for the Mutable signs, from 25-29°.

& Jupiter sextile Saturn: We have the ability to create a fortunate balance between fun and work. We may feel confident in many areas of life, as we use good judgement to make decisions that have the potential for long-term success. It is a time when we can tap into our own wisdom. Business dealings may prosper. Don't take this time for granted and let opportunities slip through your fingers. Wise and considered action. It favours the Water and Earth signs, especially those who have planets/Ascendant/ Midheaven from 4-10°.

21/6 Mercury sextile Mars: a helpful aspect to resolve practical issues. The aspect also gives determination, quick progress on the issues we want to work on, honesty in speech and technical skills. A good day for DIY. The aspect favours the Air and Fire signs especially those with planets, Ascendant or Midheaven from 15-21°.

25/6 Mercury square Neptune: a difficult aspect which can bring deception in partnerships. Cloudy judgment and confusion. Imagination is overstimulated. Intuitive thinking is more favoured. Mutable signs should be especially careful in their dealings. So are those who also have an Ascendant/Midheaven, or other planets in Mutable signs (25-29°).

26/6 Mars square Uranus: a highly adverse aspect that requires great care when driving. It can also bring mechanical problems. Beware of outbursts of violence, tensions, and nervous breakdowns and all sorts of accidents. It affects the Fixed signs from 18-24° and everyone who has planets/ Ascendant and Midheaven in those signs and degrees.

27/6 Mercury enters Cancer: Good time to communicate emotional issues. Mind is processing information based on gut or emotions. Prove to melancholy. Good time to research something related to the past. The placement activates mentally the Water and Earth signs. Capricorn, Aries and Libra might experience more tension though.

29/6 Sun trine Saturn: success in career matters but also the overcoming of difficulties. Concentration. Patience that pays off. Undertake and carry out tasks. We take control of our lives. We have more perseverance, good judgment but also reason to deal with limitations successfully. A favourable aspect for those who have planets, Ascendant/Midheaven in Water and Earth signs (especially from 4-10°).

30/6 Mercury trine Saturn: a very good aspect that favours logical thinking, organization, serious communication and generally everything that needs focus and concentration. A good time to advance business plans or attach agreements that we want to keep in time. The aspect favours the Water signs and also the Earth signs. Also favoured are those with planets, Ascendant or Midheaven in these elements (4-10°).

& Neptune stationary to turn retrograde: A period where it brings greater mental clarity, stronger intuition and messages from the subconscious. A time when we need to listen to our intuition and re-examine our issues as we may have more guidance from spiritual guides. Neptune will remain retrograde until 8th December and this retrograde period will affect those who have planets/ Ascendant or Midheaven between 24-27° of Pisces, Gemini, Sagittarius and Virgo. It will also affect in a more positive way the Water signs and Earth signs (same degrees). Signs affected may find out past deceptions against them.

1/7 Sun Conjunction Mercury: an aspect that favours mobility and also intellectual thinking. Need for communication through speech but also the need to meet up to situational demands. The aspect affects the Water signs as well as the Earth signs. It may also cause nervousness in Aries and Libra. It also affects those who have planets, Ascendant or Midheaven in all the above (5-10°).

& Mercury sextile Jupiter: A helpful aspect for traveling, teaching, and publishing. Good judgment and positive thinking. Fortunate agreements and good news. It affects the Water and Earth signs from 7-11° and those who have planets/Ascendant/Midheaven in those signs and degrees.

& Sun sextile Jupiter: An excellent aspect for luck, profits, and success. Need for expansion and travel or broadening of horizons. Favour in business. Gifts, opportunities. Favours mostly Water and Earth signs, or those with planets, Ascendant or Midheaven from 7°-11° in those signs.

2/7 Venus square Uranus: Intense social excitement. Unusual love interest or love at first sight. Unusual displays of feeling. Unconventional behaviour. Artistic rebellion. Unstable feelings. Separations and disruption in relationships. Financial losses. It affects the Fixed signs (11-13°) and those with other planets, Ascendant or Midheaven in those signs and degrees.

3/7 Full Moon in Capricorn: An amorous Full Moon with loves at first sight and explosive sexuality. The soul urges to remain grounded, but the instincts disobey. A tendency to indulge. Beware of accidents in love or business and financial situations because of our desire to break free at any cost.

7/7 Mercury sextile Uranus: A very inventive aspect. Try something new, progressive, or unusual today. An experimental attitude could spice up your life or help you resolve issues. Technical creativity and skills could be used for business or to change our everyday life for the better. It affects Earth and Water signs, or those who have planets/Ascendant/Midheaven in those signs from 19-25°.

10/7 Mercury trine Neptune: Artistic appreciation and the joys of slow living are some of the positive effects of this transit. If possible, postpone rational thinking and duties and enjoy the sea or a day in a museum. This a good aspect for artists and those who were looking for inspiration and vision in their work. It affects Water and Earth signs from 25-29° and those who have planets/Ascendant/ Midheaven in those signs and degrees.

& Mars enters Virgo: Time to be organized in order to be able to move forward. Creative solutions to problems that may have been hounding for months. You will pursue your personal desires in a practical and methodical manner. You may be critical if opposed. Good time for the signs of Earth and Water. Gemini, Sagittarius, and Pisces may have more challenging time during this transit.

& Mercury opposition Pluto: Persuasion and power in speech. A penetrating conversation might bring psychological issues to the surface. A good day for psychotherapy or research. The power of communication but be careful as this energy needs balancing to avoid conflict. Be careful with your children or pets. It affects the Cardinal signs (28-30°) and those with other planets, Ascendant or Midheaven in those signs and degrees.

11/7 Mercury enters Leo: Mind seeks fun through everyday activities. Enthusiasm in the quest for knowledge. Time to enjoy activities with children and young people. Flirting is favoured. Good time for the Fire and Air signs. Aquarius, Taurus, and Scorpio may be more restless during this transit.

15/7 Sun sextile Uranus: With this aspect, the mind becomes questioning or mentally excited. A keen interest in ideas that are progressive or innovative. A day when taking action might change things and bring improvement. Joining with others for a specific cause or purpose. The power of friendship and cooperation. It mostly affects Earth and Water signs and those who have other planets/Ascendant/Midheaven from 19-25°.

17/7 New Moon in Cancer: This Cancer New Moon brings karmic issues and relationships to the surface. Fateful relationships and a desire for total union with the other half. But timing is poor and there may be emotional blockages or emotional cruelty. It's a test of endurance.

Separations occurred are good as they release from toxic situations and liberate. Love relationships are passionate but also challenging. There might be a separation from a relationship or partnership and the opening of a new perspective.

& Mercury square Jupiter: The aspect shows an interest in learning and travel, and pushes us mentally to the limit. Judgment needs caution as mistakes can be made due to overconfidence. Otherwise, it is a favourable aspect for positive partnerships and pleasant daily life. It affects the Fixed signs and those with planets, Ascendant or Midheaven in them (8-15°).

20/7 Sun trine Neptune: The aspect usually brings, receptivity, and intuition. Good day for artists as it brings inspiration. Spend the day in solitude, by the sea, or in a museum to appreciate art. It affects Water and Earth signs from 25-29°.

& Mars opposition Saturn: This aspect is considered traditionally the aspect of bad luck. Expect some obstacles on your way and delays. Indicates bad timing. Careful with fractures, and problems with bones and teeth. It affects the Mutable signs and those with planets, Ascendant or Midheaven in them (3-9°).

22/7 Sun opposition Pluto: Sexuality and tension. Survival power. A good aspect for achieving a goal despite adversity. Makes one very competitive and requires caution with manipulation and jealousy in love relationships. Appreciate the importance of trust and sharing. This aspect can bring out unconscious behaviour which reveals underlying motives. Caution in investments. Affects the Cardinal signs or those with planets, Ascendant/ Midheaven from 27-30° in them.

23/7 Venus stationary to turn retrograde: A period to re-evaluate our love relationships, the way we give and take love and our finances. Ex partners may return or people we had intimate relationship with. It affect the Fixed signs and those who have planets, Ascendant or Midheaven in those signs (8-12°). It also affects the Fire and Air signs (8-12°). Venus will remain retrograde until 5th September. Any love decisions, marriages, or financial partnerships should wait until the retrograde period is over.

& Mercury square Uranus: another difficult aspect that requires caution in travel and transportation as it is particularly adverse. It brings damage, controversy, and tension. Beware of verbal conflicts as well. Mental overstimulation can be a benefit if used properly. It also brings sudden news related to travel, studies or contracts. Affects the Fixed signs and those with planets, Ascendant/Midheaven in them (19-25°).

27/7 Mercury conjunctions Venus: A harmonious aspect that is beneficial for social contacts, flirting, and kind interactions possibly with people from the past. Under this influence, we are more willing to compromise and agree. A good day to appreciate the beauty and express warm feelings. The aspect influences Fire and Air signs as well as those who have other planets/Ascendant or Midheaven is those signs (25-30°)

28/7 Mercury enters Virgo: This is great placement of Mercury as Virgo is the sign of its rulership. Good time for mental work that requires attention to detail. Good time to organize our daily lives more efficiently and methodically. This placement is great for the Earth and Water signs. Pisces, Gemini and Sagittarius may experience some mental tension during this time.

Available on Amazon

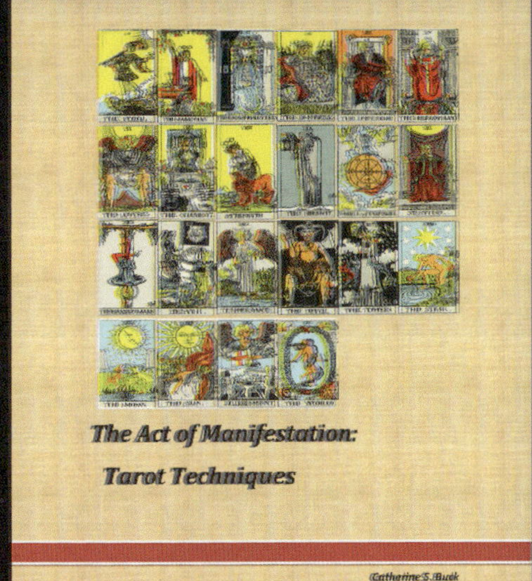

Catherine S. Buck

GRANNY BUCK'S DIBS AND DABS :

APPALACHIAN TRADITIONS AND MAGICAL WAYS

CATHERINE S. BUCK

Discover your True Self

Enchant your Life

Join the Community

An astromagical hub

ONLINE SHOP | MAGAZINES | ASTROLOGICAL SERVICES | COURSES | ONLINE EVENTS

https://imaginariumworld.co.uk
Email: imaginarium.magazine.13@gmail.com

As we have seen in previous issues, the Sun's placement in each sign gives us different characteristics and a different purpose in life.
The Sun is about our basic vitality, how we project ourselves and our consciousness. The energy of the Sun is a creative energy, radiant, with a need to exist and create, a need to be recognized and expressed. Let us now see how it is defined not only by the sign but also by the house it is in.

By Anastasia Diakidi

Sun in the 1st house

Strong " ego ", with a willingness to express it outwardly. Personality is enlightened and Aries characteristics are expressed. There is a need to be the centre of attention. They are generally very ambitious and work hard to achieve their goals and gain a good position in society. It is very important for these individuals to feel that they are distinguished and important. Sense of self-importance. Catalytic influence of the father on personality. Enthusiastic personalities, manifest themselves impulsively. The Sun in 1st house especially if it conjuncts the Ascendant indicates strong desire, abundant vitality, and great initiative and power in leadership. These people do not change their minds or desires based on others and generally have a very strong determination to follow their life path. They have abundant energy, and regenerative abilities which help them to easily overcome illnesses or physical afflictions. Caution is needed as if the Sun is afflicted in the 1st house we can see excessive pride, selfishness, false ambition, and a desire to dominate others.

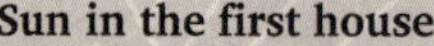
Sun in the first house

Sun in the second house

Sun in the 2nd House

Illuminating the area of finances, security, and personal value, the Sun focuses on our needs, our acquisitions, and how we will feel secure. This is a somewhat sluggish Sun that needs to develop its will and abilities in order to feel secure. It is up to the individual to learn to work, to make use of the benefits they have been gifted by the Universe and their

talents, and to understand that their financial and emotional security will depend on their effort. When they succeed, they feel successful and this increases their sense of personal worth. They need to be careful about tardiness and laziness. However, this is also a persistent, steady Sun, and if the other elements of the horoscope help, he likes the finer things in life and derives satisfaction from them.
The placement can show us that the person will acquire money or even wealth in life. The sign the Sun is in will also show us how this can be done. These individuals want to have money in order to achieve their desires and generally be financially independent. Attention is needed if this Sun is afflicted within the 2nd house as individuals may seek wealth for prestige. Caution is needed against any financial exploitation of others and also if leading a luxurious life merely for show and self-importance. There is often conservatism and stubbornness.

Sun in the 3rd House

It is a Sun most youthful and restless, whatever sign it is in. The Sun in the 3rd house shows us a strong desire for the individual to achieve distinction through intelligence and general intellectual accomplishments. Individuals have a natural curiosity and want to constantly investigate and learn new things. The sign of the Sun will show us what the individual is interested in learning. The placement also gives us a desire for travel and discovery. Ability to express and communicate their ideas is very important to them. The school years are crucial for personality development. They deal with daily affairs and their immediate environment, while siblings and neighbours play a very important role in their lives. With the Sun in the 3rd house, thinking may turn around the self and communication may be more "pompous" in the sense of focusing on the person and their personality. Also the relationship with siblings and cousins, may be characterized by paternalism. The personality gives signs of moodiness, often instability, while the person is easier to adapt to situations. Usually, there is involvement in 3rd house occupations as well, such as journalism, writing, driving, etc. There is a lot of travel and the person has the need of processing and transmitting things and ideas in some field. The father has played an important role in the development of the way of thinking. If the Sun is afflicted within the 3rd house we may see intellectual snobbery and also the tendency to impose their ideas on others.

Sun in the 4th House

A person incorporates lunar characteristics into their personality, whatever their sign. That is, they become more sensitive, attuned to the energies of others, and influenced by them. There is a strong attachment to the paternal family, home and family life, traditions, homeland, and ancestors. Natives are interested in the past and inheritance and find it difficult to leave their homes. In this placement, we see individuals who have a strong interest in ensuring security for their home and family. They are generally individuals who are very proud of their family heritage and may have a certain aristocratic outlook. Their home is usually very beautiful and has artwork. Individuals may have a property that they may even manage as a business. Individuals have a strong interest in folklore and history. Parents (especially the father) have strongly influenced the personality and the individual happily adopts this influence and even pursues it. This paternal role model, however, often becomes an obstacle to be overcome. In the early years of life, the individual may have difficulties while later in life they find security and prosperity. In the later years, the person may be able to express their core and creativity more strongly. The placement may also indicate good old age. Sensitivity and instinct, strong inner and psychological impulses that must be faced with maturity.
If the Sun is afflicted in the 4th house we may see excessive family pride, inability to get along with parents, and a tendency to impose oneself on family.

Sun in the 5th House

The Sun in the 5th house is very interested in the creation of all kinds, whether it is art, promotion, sports, family creation, and business development. These people need to be seen, "applauded" and recognized. Usually, they pursue the pleasures of life, entertainment, and promotion and "flirt" with gambling or risk-taking in some area. It is essential in this placement, to find outlets for self-expression and creative processes in order for the person to feel useful and even fulfilled. They also need love play and sex but it should not be used only as a means of gaining acceptance from others or strengthening the ego. In general, this is a Sun that can very easily fall into the trap of acting in order to gain recognition so exaggerations and the creation of a "court" that can be manipulative by taking advantage of the need for attention, should be avoided. Attention is also needed to the tendency to show off and self-referentiality which ends up tiring for others. A very important issue is children as the highest form of creation. They usually love them dearly and seek to have their own. In any case, however, people with Sun in the 5th see their creations of all kinds (it may be business, for example) as children. The sign of the Sun will give information on how and where this Sun will express itself in 5th house matters. Creative father, with Solar characteristics.
If the Sun is afflicted within the 5th house people may come out egocentric; they might lack maturity and tact, and adopt overly theatrical behaviour.

Sun in the third house

Sun in the fourth house

Sun in the 6th House

The person in this placement will be very helpful, will be in a giving mood, and will be very involved in his or her work, which very often involves service, medical

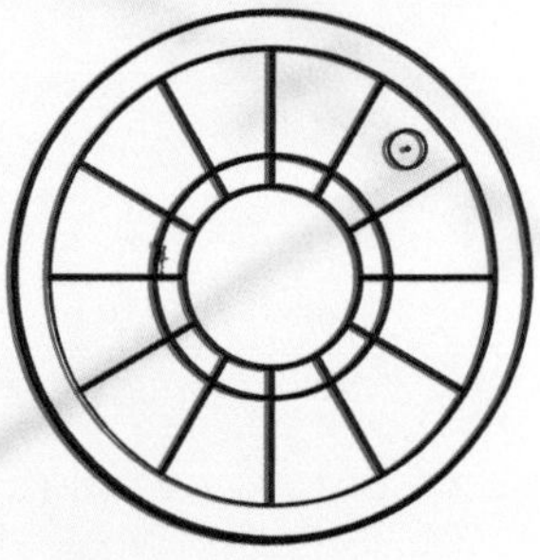

and alternative professions, but also more humble jobs. It gives a talent for organization and an appeal to "order" in general. The emphasis on attention to detail and the correction of any imperfections is typical. It gives an emphasis on food, love for small animals (unless not well placed) and a keen sense of routine. But it also gives mishaps, if it is poorly placed, and a tendency towards grumpiness and dissatisfaction. These people express themselves more easily when they are able to contribute and become indispensable in the workplace. OCD and compulsive behaviour are possible. Hypochondria can arise or in extreme cases go to the other extreme, the devaluation of body, cleanliness, and health. It is not considered one of the luckiest positions but it gives useful and hard-working people, for the most part, with a developed sense of humility. If they can overcome the obsession with perfection, they function more efficiently, without the psychological pressure resulting from a constant sense of inadequacy. Virgo father, or healer, or with a humble attitude, or with a critical attitude.
If the Sun is afflicted in the 6th house, we may see a long period of unemployment, general health, and work problems.

Sun in the 7th House

The Sun in the 7th House will be a more companionable, more cooperative Sun, with a focus on relationships, partnerships, and generally, on others. Attention is paid to outward appearance, tends to rely on others' opinions, and acts to receive acceptance. Often the professional orientation is also influenced by the 7th (lawyers, consultants, etc.) or involves professions of grooming, art, and harmony. In a female horoscope, father and husband are characterized by the 7th house and Libra themes. The need not to be lonely pushes the person into many relationships, partnerships, associations, and acquaintances. The challenge here lies in remaining true to oneself, and one's actions and decisions are defined by oneself and not to be liked by others. It gives a developed sense of justice, a talent for the arts (including that of diplomacy), and narcissistic tendencies. Difficulty in making decisions. Gives companions with Solar or Venusian characteristics. If the Sun is afflicted in the seventh house we will see problems with partners and also the tendency of these partners to impose their desires on others.

Sun in the 8th House

The Sun in the 8th house takes on the qualities and characteristics of Scorpio. This is the house of great inner quests and transformations through crises, of intensity as well as passion and so here, the psyche is profound, others take it as mysterious and "closed" and the truth is that even if they are seemingly extroverted, they hardly talk about their deeper issues unless they share them with someone with the same interests. There are many fears here including that of death, but the man is incredibly drawn to it, and as a result, manages to look it in the face and often..."defeats" it. It is considered an indicator of longevity, if well supported but also an indicator of loss of father and widowhood in a female horoscope. Father and husband Scorpio or with Plutonian occupations. Here,

Sun in the fifth house

Sun in the sixth house

Sun in the seventh house

Sun in the eighth house

there is not only interest in research or metaphysics but also involvement with it. At a lower level, however, it will give involvement with poor-quality metaphysics or "black" and dark Pluto subjects. The person in this position will come into contact with severe crises and death several times. Through these, they "kill" parts of themselves to be reborn later. There is a danger of financial parasitism as well as tendencies to control, intrigue, and scheming and manipulation. The 8th House is directly linked to libido and sex and this position gives hypersexual people but also many "vices", especially those associated with control. It gives a tendency for inheritances but also a lot of heredity in terms of health. They are tough and competitive when they feel threatened. They operate as a chameleon even in appearance, changes and transformations are part of their life. These people read energies instantly, their intuition is strong and if well supported they can influence people. Excellent position for research, psychoanalysis, biology, and surgery.
If the Sun is afflicted within the 8th house there may be recognition of the person after death. Also, there may be problems with inheritances or wills, problems with divorce, and in a female horoscope it may also indicate that her husband may lose the entire family wealth.

Sun in the 9th House

The 9th house is the house of Sagittarius and here the Sun becomes open-hearted, opening up because it loves expansions (and here the expansion is ideally mental) and any kind of knowledge or experience. The 9th gives a more optimistic view of things and the planets there don't love boundaries. So travel, philosophical pursuits, foreign cultures, and higher knowledge, are areas that will attract the Sun. Relatives, especially in-laws, will play a role in shaping the personality as will professors, but the way this Sun is placed will also show the way. Legal issues are not excluded. Travel plays a big part and if not literally, it is the travel of the mind. In a female horoscope, it gives a father or husband with Jupiter characteristics, which may also be related to foreign affairs or teaching

Photo Canva database

or intellectuals in general. Possible 9th house occupations (religion, teaching, teaching, tourism, law, publishing, writing, exports, foreign languages, etc.). Astrology also belongs here, as the science of sciences. The existence of God and the meaning of life are issues that are out of the question. Besides, here, we have to free ourselves and find the deep quests that preceded the 8th and transmit them to others.
If the Sun is afflicted in the 9th house we will see individuals trying to impose their moral and religious beliefs on others, and they may also have some eccentric beliefs. It is possible that there may also be difficulties with education or problems with foreigners or even foreign countries. The person may also have hypocritical morals. Fanaticism, adventurism, frivolity, lax morality, and troubles with the law.

Sun in the nineth house

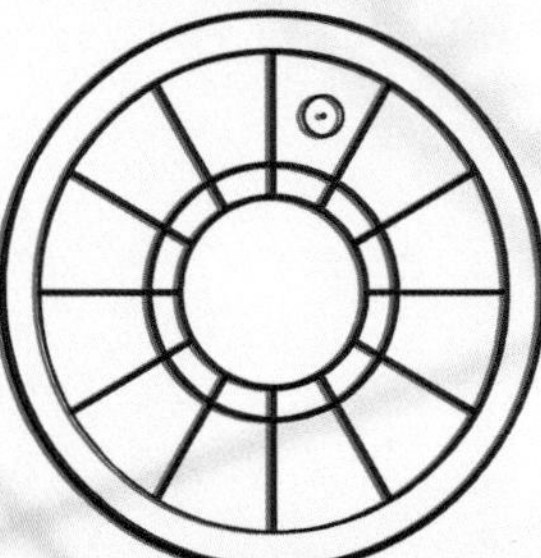

Sun in the tenth house

Sun in the 10th House

What is important here is the social and professional image, through which the individual validates his or her worth. They acquire Capricorn characteristics and thus do everything to reach the top that they have targeted in order to receive recognition. We usually see these people in a position of authority or leadership in their chosen field of work. After all, they have all the potential to achieve it and they work hard for it. What is a danger is a tendency towards authoritarianism, snobbery, and cruelty. If also the Sun is not well supported, there are difficulties in the relationship with parents. The one who has defined the personality of the person is the mother, who seems to be ambitious and dynamic but due to Sun's nature, the same may be true of the father. In a female horoscope, a strong husband or husband who holds a position of authority. Many times with this position, the individual is not expressing who they really are but what society dictates - work, etc, or the image they have of themselves, resulting in them being repressed or self-trapped in social stereotypes. Issues with authority figures and superiors, if not well supported. We may also see dictatorial tendencies and excessive love of power but also the tendency to use means to achieve their goals and rise up the hierarchy.

Sun in the 11th House

The Sun in the 11th house, acquires a Aquarian spirit and turns towards groups, associations, and movements. Natives are interested in the common good and often due to their involvement with trade unionism, they turn to politics, in which there is always an interest but at a level that concerns the whole and social reforms. Of great importance are the friendly relations by which they not only influence but also structure the personality. They are always available for their friends unless the Sun is afflicted. In that case, we will see the kind of blockages that can be caused by them. It might indicate the tendency to dominate friends for selfish purposes. The negative manifestation of the position is related to rebel without reason or cause, or the inability to manifest and support new goals and hopes. They are interested in issues of technology and have innovative ideas almost always with the common good in mind. Caution is also needed in absolutist ideologies which can be fanatically supported. The father may also bring together many of the above characteristics, be Aquarian or Uranian, involved in technology, politics, or alternative therapies. Interest in astrology or even opposition to anything outside the sphere of their perception.

Sun in the 12th House

The 12th house is a "mysterious" house, unclear. It is where hidden situations take place, but it is also where the person hides what he or she does not want to face. The Sun there finds it difficult to understand and express itself and has difficulty in discerning who others really are as well. It tends to create imaginary situations, creating a world of their own.
The placement shows a blurred picture in terms of the father figure, or father "lost", or frustrating - hidden situations with the partner in a female sign. Women in this placement are attracted to partners who may have addictions, or the nature of the relationship is unclear or involved in complicated situations. Father and partner of Pisces nature, or father and partner who have a sacrificial attitude. Individuals in this placement are hypersensitive, and unless this sensitivity is led to the relief of others or engagement in art and metaphysics, it is eventually turned against the self who withdraws in frustration into their own world. As a house associated with hidden enemies, it often puts the individual in the position of having to negotiate betrayals and disappointments. The person has leadership tendencies behind the scene. May also indicate self-expression through large institutions such as asylums, prisons, and hospitals. They are very interested in places since they can retreat and generally have metaphysical tendencies. Through giving they find fulfilment. If the Sun is afflicted in the 12th house, we may see neurotic tendencies as well as excessive shyness. Beware as individuals may control others through secret means. It is possible that the mystical involvement stems from egoism and the desire for power and recognition. Individuals may have powerful secret enemies but may also be subconsciously their own worst enemies.

Sun in the eleventh house

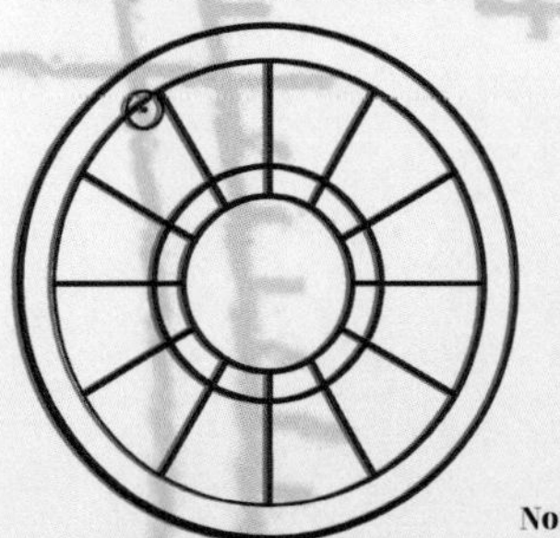

Sun in the twelfth house

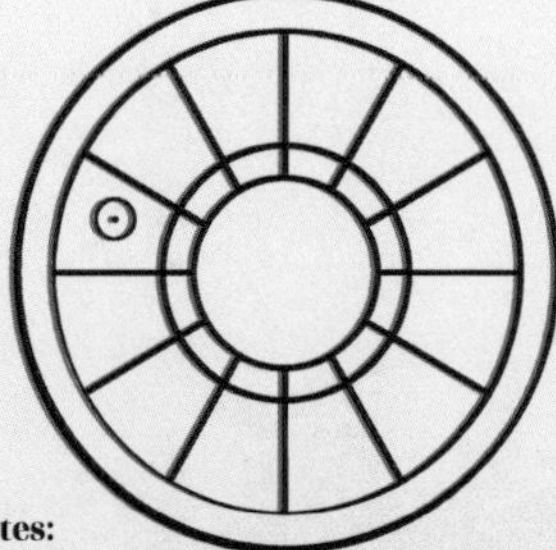

Notes:
From the lessons with a great teacher, the late Helena Menegou.

Intention Setting With Tarot

New Moon Intention Setting

BY JESSICA SMITH

The new moon is an exciting time of new beginnings and fresh starts. It is a time where we reflect and check in on ourselves and our lives, think about habits we want to cultivate or projects we want to grow.

Sometimes it is easy to think of our intentions but other times we may need some help to think below the surface. We can use the tarot to help us intention set. Tarot cards can illuminate areas of our lives that may need some nurture or attention that may not be immediately obvious to us.

An intention is not a goal. Goals are concrete achievements which can be measurable, whereas an intention is the journey you go on to achieve your goal. For example, your goal might be to be able to confidently hold a tricky yoga inversion. Your intention would be to practice yoga daily and concentrate on strengthening poses required in order to achieve the pose.

Creating Space
Physically and mentally

What puts many people off about rituals is the perceived elaborateness and aesthetic that is required. Instagram may have you believing that you need lots of beautiful crystals, large candles and bundles of beautifully wrapped sage for a successful new moon ceremony. You don't. You need 20 minutes alone time (any time of day, anywhere in the house), a journal and your cards. You don't even need to be bang on the new moon. Ritual just means a habit that we perform with reverence.

Find some time where you wont be disturbed around the time of the new moon. It is best to come to set your new moon intentions in the right frame of mind. If you have jobs to do or things niggling you then do these first. If you're not feeling up to it, do a self care activity instead. However, don't avoid sacred time because you're not feeling serene, calm and centred- when does this ever happen? Come as you are.

Set the space in any way that feels natural to you. It might be lighting a candle, working in a special space or just spending a few moments breathing in and out and letting your body get used to the change of pace. The more we do these things the quicker our body gets into this state.

The Power of Journaling

I cannot stress enough the benefits of keeping a regular journal. The act of journaling helps to clear the mind, assimilate our thoughts and helps us to start to delve little deeper into our subconscious, as well as being a beautiful way to document your life. Spend a few minutes writing down your current thoughts and feelings, see this as a release of your emotions and thoughts, clearing the way for clear thinking and opening up your intuition.

Now think about what you are grateful for. When we practice gratitude, we raise our vibration making it easier to manifest the life we want. Gratitude has also been proven to improve mood and mental health. You can meditate on what you're feeling grateful for, journal your thoughts or simply write a list of 3 things.

The next exercise may seem like an odd one but it can be a very powerful way to manifest. In your journal, and crucially in the present tense, write about the life you want. This could be your entire life or just a part of it. Write as though you are telling someone what your life is like, document your feelings, your daily activities, your relationships and your material possessions and finances. This helps us to see the bigger picture and creates the energy needed to help the tarot direct your intentions.

Choosing the Cards

Now it's time to use our cards! Hold your cards in your hands, close your eyes and ask the question:

"what intentions should I be setting in order to manifest the life I want?"

Shuffle in any way that is natural to you and select a card intuitively. Look at the card and study it. Don't immediately jump to keywords in your head. Study the image, what can you see? What is the energy of the card? What is happening? What might the colours mean? What action, if any, is there in the image? Consider the suit as this may give you a clue as to the area of your life the intention should be for. If you select a major arcana card then the message is stronger, this may be an intention that requires extra attention or one that may need more than one month's moon cycle to embed.

When you have studied the card, begin to journal your thoughts and feelings that have arisen from looking at the image. Don't think too much about this, you may be surprised by what you start to write when you let go.

If you've done this first step and feel you need more clarity, then use your little white book or google to find more information about the card- but be discerning. Your intuition knows best. Be critical but unjudgmental of yourself. However, don't explore a card to death. If you pick a card and it depicts a garden and you know this means for you to spend more time in your own garden, then go with this. Don't search for more meaning. If you really can't decipher a card, record it anyway and come back to it after a few days, it may become clear as events unfold.

Writing Your Intention

Now that you have selected a card and understood the meaning, it's time to write your intention. Use positive language and focus on what you intend to do rather than not do. For example "I wont snap at my children" becomes "I will speak with positivity and kindness to my children". "I wont eat junk food" becomes "I will eat healthy and nourishing food".

Once you are happy with your intentions record them in your journal. You may want to speak them out loud to affirm them to yourself and the universe. You will need to refer to them regularly so they stay in the forefront of your mind. You could keep them as a note on your phone or stick a post it note on your mirror.

Suits

Pentacles
home, finances, material belongings, health

Swords
mental state, learning, communicating

Wands
passion, motivation, energy, creativity

Cups
relationships, emotions, mood

The end of the ceremony is the perfect time for a little relaxation. This could be a simple guided meditation, some yoga nidra or visualisation. When you are finished, thank yourself for allowing yourself this time.

Photo Canva Stock

In the early Florentine Renaissance, a Humanist philosopher, priest and astrologer named Marsilio Ficino developed a contemplation method to alleviate his suffering of depression. He used uplifting positive allegorical images as a therapeutic tool to heal or "cure" his melancholia. Ficino taught the elite members of his Hermetic Academy to encourage the positive aspects of our higher selves by interacting and contemplating beautiful images.

People have been trying to understand themselves and have struggled with emotional maladies throughout history, and although the world has changed dramatically, we are still dealing with the same human emotions. I like that the neoclassical allegorical images that also appear in Tarot cards from that era have been helping people do this for hundreds of years and that they are still relevant.

I've always believed that Tarot symbolism speaks to the subconscious mind in a very significant and helpful way. So, when my client asked "do you have to know the Tarot to do the Ten of Wands meditation you described in your Best Tarot Practices book" (my book features guided visualization as helpful and therapeutic for the Major Arcana, selected Minors including challenging cards) I thought what a brilliant question. She'd read my visualization instructions and was moved to perform the meditation because she felt as if she was carrying the weight of others' problems as well as her own, "like the person in the card picture."

Her concern revolved around the visualization process helping her if she didn't know all the relationships between the intricate card symbolism and interpretive meanings. The woman's intuitive subconscious recognized the significance of the meditation-visualization; she wanted to do the contemplation without learning the entire Tarot.

Yes, you can participate in creative Tarot visualization without a full understanding of the card's symbolism. When a Tarot visual "speaks to you" or resonates with you it is a sure sign that you are meant to create an imaginative dialogue with it. Although seemingly unusual and unpleasant, contemplation of a perceived negative card is really the courageous ability to confront a life challenge and remove obstacles of inauthenticity.
Another reason to dialogue with a specific card is its appearance in a helping influence placement in a reading's layout. You can also choose to contemplate a Tarot card image to open a

passageway to its secret wisdom and positivity. Once you've experienced the Tarot's imaginative self awareness feature you will retain the card meaning, guaranteed.

The Ten of Wands

Traditionally The Ten of Wands is a challenging card that depicts an overburdened figure oppressed with too many wands, staffs or rods that are carried on their back. It will often represent someone who has shouldered many responsibilities that may or may not be theirs to carry.

Uncomfortable and stressed, my client sensed the visual method I described for the card could help her. She intuited that because the Tarot symbolism speaks to the subconscious mind, it would reveal what she needed to understand and what action to take during her contemplation session. Often times the imaginative approach will present knowledge in the best way to understand a message. In her case, she named, discarded, revised and repackaged the bundle of wands.

The idea of choice she discovered was revolutionary for her; as was engaging with the soul aspect of the Tarot visuals as a pathway to a better life. She ended up in therapy where her therapist shared a phrase that became her mantra motto "not my monkey, not my circus." I could see the "monkey on her back" and its similarity to the heavy bundle of wands carried by the card's figure clear as day. The final outcome was she learned how to manage responsibilities to others, how to say no, how to remain centered and how to be true to her own self.

The Self-awareness healing side of the Tarot experience.

When it comes to healing and contemplation, I like to see how the client responds to my abstract light images in my new Spirit Light Tarot cards. This time there is no symbolism to focus upon, instead colour, patterns and shapes are used and they allow for a deep immediate dive, becoming messengers from the client's soul.

A card is chosen then I simply ask about the what they perceive is happening in the picture, there is no right or wrong, just increased awareness. Topics are color attraction, energy movement, feelings, what does it remind you of? Sensation is now included; how is it felt and where in the body - left, right, top, base, front or back, in chakras, aura, is there movement - ingress or egress, how does it feel - relaxing, invigorating, grounding etc. you can then use this information for guided visualization and healing.

This is powerful because the information comes from the client and you are the guide or facilitator rather than the interpreter and diviner. As a healer you can use their description by focussing on the person's chakras, energy field and aura with specific directions from the client's higher self received via their contemplation. The same method applies when working solo.

How to use The Spirit Light Tarot Cards for self-awareness or with a client.

Elaine was a healer, medium and psychic seeking inner peace. As her spiritual advisor I knew she sincerely aspired toward the personal every day well-being that springs from conscious connection with her soul. Known by many names, it is the quest and desire for self awareness, self actualization, the higher self, divine mind, spiritual love, infinite intelligence and spirituality. Tarot contemplation is a way to connect with that source.

The Tarot Contemplation Process - During our session she was attracted to The Star.
My description from The Spirit Light Tarot Card Booklet –

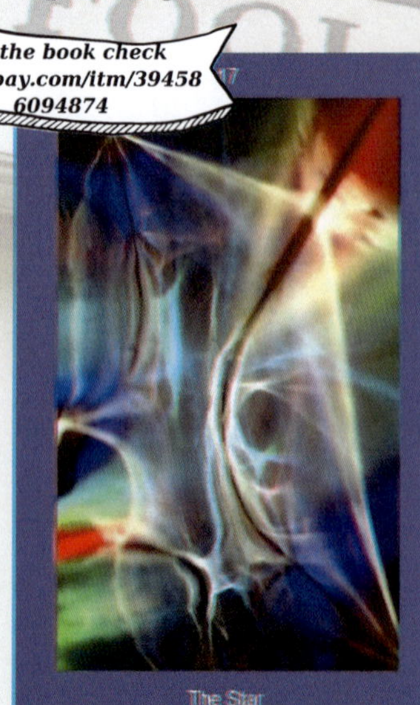

"The Star - Stars beam light toward each other creating an interplay between them. Colorful lights flow and create shapes, they represent the layers of the multi-dimensional realm represented by The Star Card experience. Deep universal blue, turquoise and white

harmonizes with the opposite color – orange, along with green, the color of balance, hope and healing. The colors all remain distinct while making a beautiful multi colored mystical everchanging tapestry.
The card design illustrates the ethereal network circuitry between the individual nature and the eternal self that becomes highlighted through meditation practices.
The image features direct light beams and small white and blue stars that represent the chakras."

I placed the Spirit Light Tarot Star card in front of her after she had performed a centering meditation of simple breathing. The image was new to her, she opened her eyes and after a few moments responded to the card's shapes and patterns. The energy within the shapes and their directional movement grabbed her attention. For her The Star card had stars that were sending light from above to below and back again in a stream of light beams. She commented, "Oh, I see, this is a pathway from the divine world to the human and back again." She studied the image then continued, "the energy is warm and I want an invitation to that pathway."

It was clear that Elaine wanted to deepen her connection with "the divine world" and she intuited that it would feel like a warm homecoming. Then she revealed how she could gain access into it.

"The colors are very inviting too," referencing a second look more studious approach to The Star. She spent a long time with the colors, each one had a special meaning to her and that is how Elaine developed her psychic color repertoire to use for healing and giving spiritual readings. "I was taught to create a personal psychic color dictionary. If a color came into my third eye (clairvoyance) to use in a certain area of a person's body, I would send (channel or transmit) it for healing purposes."

The spontaneous flow continued, "when I first decided I wanted to learn about the Tarot, I would study the card and read the book. Then, I learned to look at the card and see what parts of the card popped out at me. I looked at it first for the colors. I would get a psychic impression based on the color and that's how I started the reading for the client." She was actually already practising the intuitive Tarot visualization approach!

As she reminisced and revealed her unique intuitive process, she was also reconnected to her essential spiritual nature, all because she took the time to look at and contemplate one Spirit Light Tarot card.

It was clear that she could use the energy guidance she saw in the image for further meditation and personal healing and was advised to take action by going within and allowing herself to embrace and value all the aspects she mentioned.

Elaine now had an understanding that the inner peace she was seeking was already present within her. (Often clients are seeking something outwardly that really is within.) Her responses revealed the route to her goal as she reconnected with her multitude of spiritual aptitudes and gifts (the meaning of The Star card.) In her outer life teaching became her way forward.

Tarot visualization is clearly another memorable way to connect with the cards. This practice requires looking at the chosen card, then following guided instructions. As the figures and atmosphere comes to life new insightful connections are made. By performing (or even reading about them) you can turn a perceived negative card into a positive lesson and an allegorical archetype into a channel for the gods. If you are seeking more ways to help yourself, clients and students this is a great technique to add to your Tarot repertoire with remarkable insightful results. A Tarot card can transport you into the past and the future, into the subconscious and the soul it will make you a cartomancer and also a facilitator of healing.

Marcia began her metaphysical career early. She co-owned a tea room, bookstore and had a daily radio talk show featuring the occult, new age and astrology. Because she encountered many clients and listeners from all walks of life seeking guidance, she developed an easy-to-understand metaphysical vernacular for her tarot and astrology readings including a blend of astrology and tarot interpretation designed to help and guide each person. Marcia wrote two best seller books on the Tarot, Easy Tarot Guide and Best Tarot Practices, both available on Amazon and through your local bookseller. She is the creator of two limited edition Tarot Decks - The Spirit Light Tarot and The Fountain of Light Tarot as well as The Lily Dale Oracle cards inspired by Spiritualism. Her current projects include The New Spirit Light Tarot Deck and she has branched out into mainstream writing with a metaphysical twist.

Contact marciamasinoastrotarotart@yahooo.com
https://mmasino.wixsite.com/tarotbooks

Using Tarot to Aid Your Daily Spiritual Practice

Tarot is a tool to help us discover ourselves, deeper parts of ourselves, how we think, uncover thoughts we didn't know we had, illuminate triggers and sticking points. We can use it for advice and guidance, to help us make decisions and to support us when we need it. The act of using tarot helps us to develop our intuition which then makes our daily lives more connected and in flow. Being able to trust ourselves, being more decisive and helping us to keep our wits about us.

A Morning Practice

A morning routine calms our nervous system and grounds us for the day ahead. Any morning routine will do this. The essence of a daily practice is to support us in returning to a state of balance. It is an act of self care- we are important enough for this. I find it sets my tone for the day, hopefully one of serenity and gratitude, and allows us to set an intention for the day. We tune into the energy of the day, the energy of ourselves, helping us to feel into what we might need.

Sacred Space

Many people who have a daily mindfulness or journaling practice will like to create a sacred space to do this in. This isn't necessary but by having a familiar space that resonates helps us to connect with our intuition quicker. You could do this by having a special chair, a table of objects, perhaps candles, plants, crystals. Maybe some images or pictures displayed. You might play music. When pulling cards it's useful to make sure you have quiet and you won't be disturbed so you can tap more easily into your intuition.

Daily Card Pull

It's a nice idea to get into the habit of ensuring you are working within a high vibration when working with tarot. It isn't always necessary with a daily card pull but for anything more than this I would recommend doing so. We work in a high vibration to ensure we are only working in an atmosphere of calmness and love. This keeps us protected and ensures we feel uplifted and secure, even if dealing with subject matter that isn't. Simple ways to raise our vibration and vibration around us: lighting a candle or incense, playing nice music, breathwork and visualisation.

Take a few deep breaths to calm and ground yourself, clearing your mind of any unnecessary thoughts. Shuffle the cards until you feel intuitively called to stop and then choose the top card. Study the card carefully before diving straight for a book of meanings. Try not to let any keywords of the card cloud your judgement at first, study the image, How does it make you feel, do you feel drawn to anything. It is this initial process we must learn to trust. Once you have studied the card, you can look up its meaning and then journal any thoughts and feelings you have. It is a good idea to record the card even if you're not journaling about it. This way you can keep an eye on patterns and repeats.

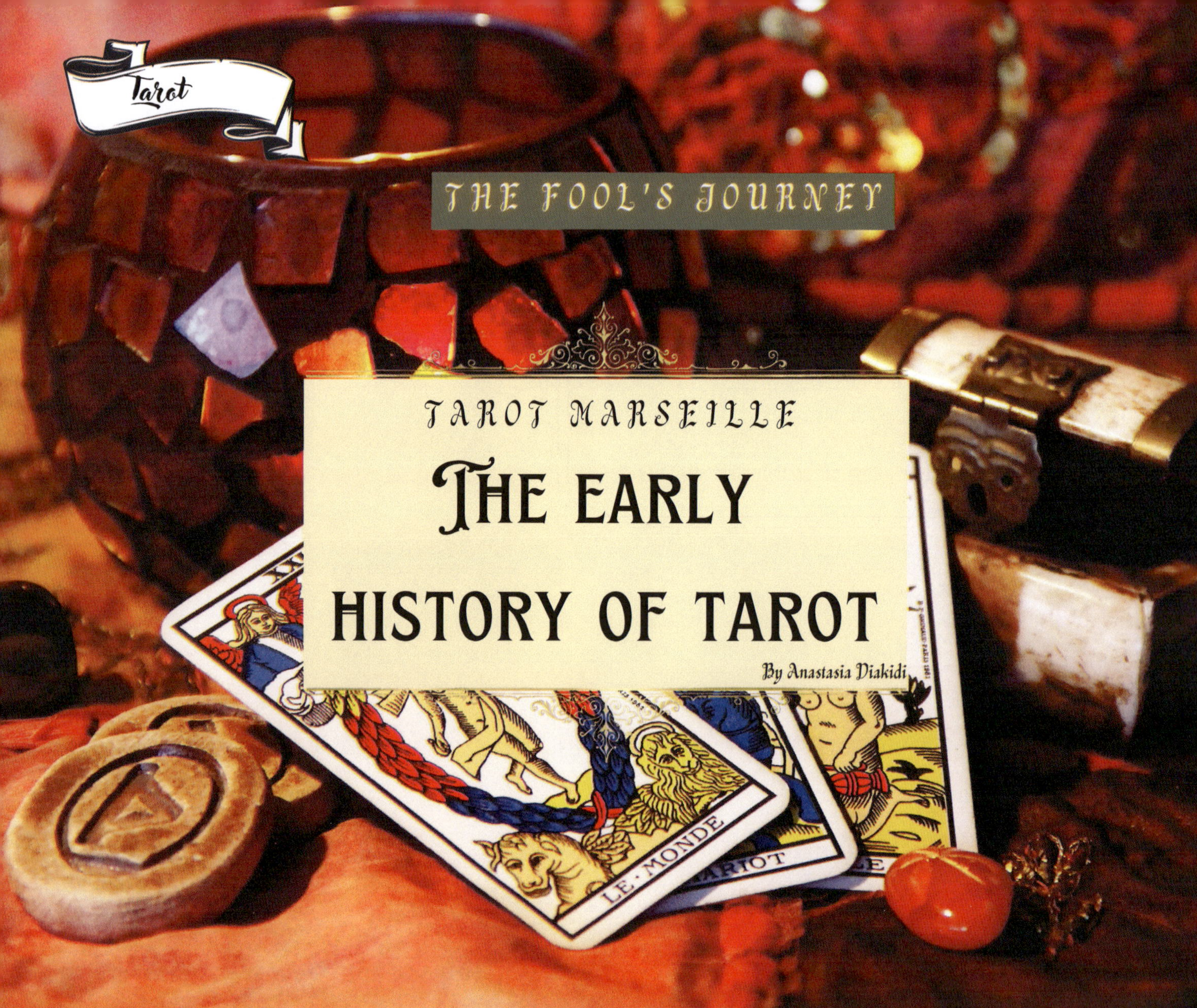

TAROT MARSEILLE

THE EARLY HISTORY OF TAROT

By Anastasia Diakidi

Tarot appeared as a card game throughout Europe in the 18th and 19th centuries. At the time, Tarot was considered a fun card game, so decks were generally used for that purpose rather than for esoteric purposes. Whatever their use, Tarot cards attracted the interest of master printers, who in turn brought new levels of artistry and craftsmanship to the decks. Inspired to produce their own versions of the cards, these printmakers had an outstanding impact on Tarot history. The most successful deck of the era was the Marseille, a French deck of the early 18th century. The images that appear on this classic deck date back to the 18th century, when they were engraved on special wood blocks for printing. These blocks were used by the printer for over a century in various editions, using different combinations of colours and paper.

Despite the rapid changes in the countries that adopted the Marseille model, it remained fairly stable in terms of its illustrations and card numbering. It was so popular that it became the standard Tarot illustrative style of the time, serving as a model deck for other manufacturers.

The Marseille Tarot can be considered the ancestor of all modern decks of cards. The symbolic cards of the 19th century have their origin in these cards, as well as the illustrated, intuitive decks of the 20th and 21st centuries. The name Marseille refers to the place where the iconographic model for the cards was made, not the place where they were printed. Historically, the French city of Marseille was one of the most important centres of Tarot card production. It is believed that the cards were introduced to France by soldiers after their invasion of the Italian city of Milan in 1499. The Marseille Tarot, first printed in France in 1751, is a classic deck of cards featuring well-defined and simple images. However, the design of the Arcana de Marseille is likely to have been inspired by the Italian Tarot created during the Renaissance.

There are many Marseille decks of cards, with slight variations in design, symbolism, and colours. Early issues of the Marseilles Tarot bear the initials of the printer and any tax stamps, usually on the Ace.

I
BATEL
XI
LA FO
XXI
LE·MO
VII
LE CHARIO

The Marseille deck has a traditional Tarot structure, divided into 22 Major Arcana and 56 Minor Arcana. Compared to the images, symbolism, and illustrations of modern decks, the cards may seem unsophisticated. The designs are plain, and the numbered Minor Arcana cards are without special illustrations, with only basic figures arranged in precise geometric shapes.

The geometry and design of the cards can be a source of inspiration in interpretation, but the structural elements of the deck - the number and suit - are much more important. In particular, odd-numbered cards are considered "active" (known as male) and even-numbered cards are considered "reflective" (female). In the Major Arcana, the Tarot of Marseilles also contains a profusion of deep symbolism beneath what may appear to be simplistic images and depictions of characters or actions. The abstract nature of the cards can allow the reader to free themselves from any predetermined meaning and arrive at an authentic, personal interpretation. The cards start from the basic presumption that each image expresses more than a simple meaning and nothing is exclusively good or bad. Each image encompasses the duality of life: good and evil, light and darkness, birth and death, day and night. This means that the cards cannot be understood and interpreted "by the book" alone. The Reader must use their intuition.

The iconographic model of the Tarot of Marseille has endured through the centuries, despite changes throughout Europe. The cards that changed most frequently in the Marseilles decks were those with political or religious significance. Religious conflicts between Catholics and Protestants throughout Europe in the second half of the 18th century probably led many printers to replace some cards. For example, Juno replaced the High Priestess in Jean Jerger's Tarot (early 19th century, Besançon). In Adam De Hautot's Tarot (c. 1740, Rouen), the High Priestess is replaced by Captain Fracasse.

Jean-Baptiste Galler's Tarot of the Devil (18th century, Brussels) is an example of a variation on the Marseille model. The iconography is inspired by the Tarot of Bologna, suggesting that the Tarot, even in the 18th century, was open to outside influences.

However, at the beginning of the 19th century, the original models returned and new versions of the Tarot began to appear.

Meanwhile, the commercial success of the Marseilles Tarot led to improvements in artistic techniques that enhanced production and quality, as well as lowering costs. This promoted the popularity of the cards and also increased accessibility.

Colours give added significance to the cards in the Marseille Tarot deck:

White: wisdom, purity, peacefulness
Black: the end of things
Red: active energy, passion, creativity
Yellow: vital energy, Divine Mind
Green: nature and all creation
Blue: receptive energy, spirit and mind
Blue sky: elements of the air, lucidity, clarity
Flesh: human beings and physical reality

The Marseille Tarot was eventually adopted by modern occultists in France and England, helping to transform the Tarot from a simple card game into a form of divination and cartomancy.

The Tarot of Marseille remains to this day one of the most commercial decks of cards and is considered timeless. It is - together with Waite's deck - a classic choice, especially for those who do not want to adopt the modern elements of Tarot's contemporary illustrations.

The Marseille Tarot was eventually adopted by modern occultists in France and England, helping to transform the Tarot from a simple card game into a form of divination and cartomancy.

The Cups

The cups associated with the element of water represent the feminine principle and often indicate issues related to feelings and emotions, pleasure, sensitivity, but also marriage, and love. Of the four suits the cups are considered the lucky one and to see several of them in a reading is a very favourable sign.

Photo Canva database

ACE

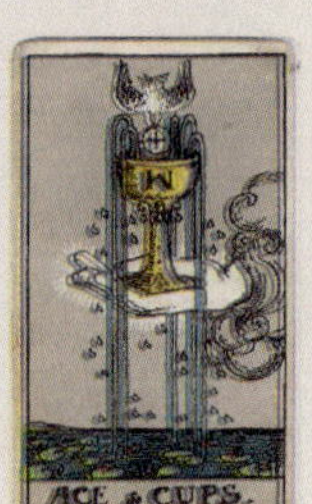

A very favourable card that often indicates the beginning of a relationship or a creative venture. The card shows us that we are connected to our spirit, heart, and soul. It often indicates intuition and also the virtue of forgiveness. It can show us that the lover is searching for the meaning of life. The card directs us to express our feelings and to be in touch with them in general. In a love reading, it can show the beginning of new love, new bonds, the feelings that are evolving but also the deeper desire for connection. Ace of Cups can also denote a pregnancy.

In a career reading, Ace of Cups signifies work in the beauty industry, tourism, and hospitality. The Ace of Cups tarot card also speaks of spiritual and artistic work.

TWO

The card is associated with cooperation and partnership, especially when seen in a career reading. More generally, it symbolizes giving and receiving love and support, and the card may also suggest spiritual love or healing love. The card speaks of reaching out to each other, romantic love, and also sexual attraction as an alchemical merging of two people; creating a union of harmony, understanding, and cooperation. Many times we will also see it indicate reconciliation or forgiveness.

In a career reading, Two of Cups signifies work in hospitality, wine taster, therapist, and healer. Two of Cups can also mean you will find love at work.

THREE

The card symbolizes team spirit and friendship in general. In one reading it can show a celebration, friends, and general popularity in social circles. If we see this card it means that we may be enjoying our social circle, making friends, or joining a group where we can now share beautiful feelings with others. It generally symbolizes team spirit and trust. If it does not denote a specific celebratory ceremony, the card can signify abundance and healing on a more abstract level.

In a career reading, the Three of Cups card signifies work-related events and colleagues who also are your friends. Three of Cups can also denote fun jobs in hospitality, tourism, and event planning.

FOUR

The card has a hint of satisfaction and dissatisfaction. It shows us that what is high will often fall. We will often see the card as a sign that we are uninspired or generally feeling bored. It may indicate that we are busy with our own issues or that we want to be left alone to think. It is possible, of course, that others have left us out. The card encourages us to find time to work on ourselves without being permanently preoccupied with ourselves and ignoring others. It can indicate meditation for therapeutic purposes. But it advises us not to take things personally, not to remain apathetic and passive. It is important not to question yourself but also not to overlook what is in front of you and what life has to offer. The card may indicate that you are hurt and defensive and withdrawn.

In a career reading, the Four of Cups card signifies complacency in work. The Seeker knows how to do their work well, but doesn't love it enough to be really good at it.

FIVE

The card speaks of the pain of loss. Somehow we are hurt when this card is shown or that we are emotionally unfulfilled. Pay attention to not just focus on the negative as it can show that we are generally difficult to satisfy ourselves too. The card shows bitterness and sadness but also regret for some missed opportunities. Definitely a card of emotional instability advising you to accept things as they are and not to emotionally resist change. Change your priorities instead of wishing the past could be changed.

In a career reading, Five of Cups card signifies work that doesn't really satisfy the Seeker. The Seeker might have great potential to achieve in career, but for some reason is unable to blossom. It can also mean the Seeker feels isolated at work.

SIX

The card symbolizes innocence, childhood, and nostalgia for the past. Through this card, we see the simple joys of life, childishness, and kindness. We feel at home and home is certainly where our heart is. It is also a card of goodwill and good intentions towards others. The card has a connection to the past and can indicate emotional memories, feelings of nostalgia, and reminiscing. In a love reading, it can indicate a relationship that is light and playful or one that brings out the child in you. The card also indicates naivety or innocence, sharing, and reconciliation.

In a career reading, Six of Cups signifies feeling at home with work and feeling safe at work and with the people you work with. Six of Cups card can also mean careers in childcare and hospitality or work that involves delving into the past, such as a historian or investigator.

SEVEN

The card shows that we are emotionally empty and that we often want to escape from reality. In a career reading, it can also indicate time management and disorganization or a general lack of organization in the professional environment. It can also be a sign of laziness or procrastination. Caution is needed the card can also show high expectations or even fantasies of what you can have without doing much to achieve it. In a love reading, it may show the illusions about love or a range of options available to you.

EIGHT

The card speaks of a change of direction and urges us to follow our dreams and search for deeper meaning. The card may indicate that we are focusing more on the spiritual realm than the material, and it is possible that the card also indicates that we are abandoning the mainstream way of life.

In a love reading, it may indicate that we are emotionally distant or that we are generally withdrawing from a situation or relationship. It is a loneliness card but it always shows that we are moving on to something better.

The card can also indicate a journey to discover ourselves or to seek a spiritual or emotional truth. It is favourable when you want to move away from the past and leave a difficult situation behind.

In a career reading, Eight of Cups can also mean pursuing what the Seeker always wanted to do, but was too afraid to do.

Photo Canva Stock

NINE

The card indicates that you are proud of yourself or that you have found purpose and meaning in your life. It generally indicates the pleasures of life, and may also indicate that you live in luxury. Definitely, a card that shows that you are on the path you desire and take pleasure in the simple pleasures of life or all that you have achieved. With this card, your desires in both the love and professional areas are fulfilled. As a piece of advice, it is important to be grateful for what you have achieved, and motivates you not to remain complacent as you have now achieved everything you want.

TEN

The card shows idealistic values but also being aligned with our true nature. As a card, it shows the happy ending. In a love reading, it could indicate that we finally have a beautiful relationship like we never had before. It indicates emotional fulfilment in a romantic commitment and also shows that the ideals of love are now attainable.

The card also symbolizes a sense of oneness with the world and finally speaks of the completion of a cycle and also the restoration of order.

In a career reading, Ten of Cups denotes careers in the public eye, creative jobs, and property investments. Ten of Cups in a career reading can also mean the Seeker has found the perfect job.

PAGE

The card may show a handsome young man usually of a fair complexion.
It may be someone offering you love or romance, a young lover.

Like all pages, he speak of messages and in this case, it is a romantic message or a confession. It is a card that shows the romance, an admirer flirting with you. It can also show the beginning of an affair. Generally, the card motivates you to show your feelings.

In a professional reading, it may indicate an audition or the showcasing of your talents generally that you are creative and learning a new creative skill. A card related to creative ideas trust in intuition and imagination.

KNIGHT

The knight shows a person with strong idealism, emotional sensitivity, quite volatile as a person who is often in love with love and likes challenges in the romantic arena. A person generally inventive but without realism. He is emotionally expansive and loves beauty.

The card shows the manifestation of love or affection. It often shows that we may be wearing rose-tinted glasses about a love affair or seeing the situation with too much emotion or too much optimism. It may also show that we are rushing to save someone because we are generally too diffuse with our emotions.

In a professional reading, it can indicate an artist, a business trip, or generally a creative phase at work. You may need to put on a performance or entertain an audience.

QUEEN

The Queen is a compassionate woman, quite affectionate and emotionally awakened. She is an honest, often fair-skinned woman who has good character and is generally easy-going and calm. A woman with enough intuition to understand the underlying emotional currents in the atmosphere.

The card shows that we use our imagination to create something, while also making others feel comfortable and beautiful. The card can also show self-improvement in some areas. The trap of this card is not to judge ourselves too much by over-loving others. It is important to know our limits as the card also indicates unconditional love.

In a love reading, it could show that we are a magnet for a new romance, that we have generally achieved emotional harmony with our partner and have patience and calmness in our relationship.

In a professional reading, it could show a willingness to support people who work with or for us.

KING

The card could show us a fair-skinned man in a position of responsibility who is quite wise, diplomatic, and generous.

In general, the card symbolizes stability, support, generosity, wisdom, and diplomacy. It shows that we are emotionally strong and generally lovable as individuals and others can rely on us. It also indicates that we may have adopted an altruistic lifestyle as well.

In a business reading, it may show that we have the wisdom as well as the good judgment to act in a controlled manner and evaluate situations correctly.

In a love reading, it shows emotional security but also acceptance of our partner's limits. In general, it can show the balanced atmosphere within the relationship.

Photo Canva Stock

Ancient Wisdom

THE ORPHIC HYMN TO APOLLO

Blest Pæan, come, propitious to my pray'r,
Illustrious pow'r, whom Memphian tribes revere,
Slayer of Tityus, and the God of health,
Lycorian Phœbus, fruitful source of wealth.
Spermatic, golden-lyr'd, the field from thee

Receives it's constant, rich fertility.
Titanic, Grunian, Smynthian, thee I sing,
Python-destroying, hallow'd, Delphian king:
Rural, light-bearer, and the Muse's head,
Noble and lovely, arm'd with arrows dread:

Far-darting, Bacchian, two-fold, and divine,
Pow'r far diffused, and course oblique is thine.
O, Delian king, whose light-producing eye
Views all within, and all beneath the sky:
Whose locks are gold, whose oracles are sure,

Who, omens good reveal'st, and precepts pure:
Hear me entreating for the human kind,
Hear, and be present with benignant mind;
For thou survey'st this boundless Æther all,
And ev'ry part of this terrestrial ball.

Abundant, blessed; and thy piercing sight,
Extends beneath the gloomy, silent night;
Beyond the darkness, starry-ey'd, profound,
The stable roots, deep fix'd by thee are found.
The world's wide bounds, all-flourishing are thine,

Wherefore you bear the formative seal of the entire Cosmos.
Hear, happy one, my supplicating voice, thus saving the initiates!

Gift Ideas by IMAGINARIUM

For Modern Witches!

Visit

www.imaginariumworld.co.uk

Beauty & Home Products

100% natural

Ethical

Eco

Notebooks - Journals - Planners

Your words have power to change your day, your life, the world!

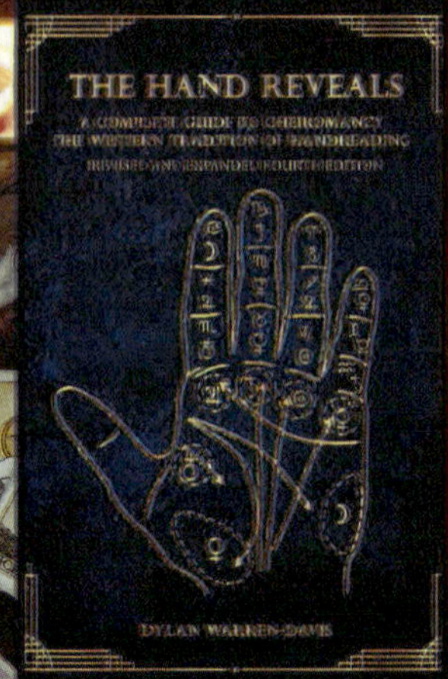

WHEN STARS COLLIDE

PAUL WESTRAN

Books

Enchanting authors share their 'magic'!

Printed in Great Britain
by Amazon